Acclaim for Felix Dennis
[and a couple of brickbats]

"He writes like a man obsessed… If Waugh were still alive, he would fall on Dennis's verse with a glad cry of recognition and approval."
— **John Walsh,** *The Independent*

"The unpredictable Felix Dennis, long known for publishing other things, now bursts forth as a 21st century Kipling. In the poor old mallarme'd and ezrapounded world of contemporary poetry, no poet is taken seriously if he rollicks and rolls with rhyme, meter, and melody and can be understood in fewer than four read-throughs. But the Kipling of Barrack-Room Ballads and The Recessional could not be denied, at long last, despite decades of fashionable vituperation. Kipling II, I predict, will be just as much trouble — which he enjoys making on stage as well as on page."
— **Tom Wolfe,** author

"I enjoy his poetry immensely…"
— **Mick Jagger,** singer, songwriter

"Shakespeare beware. Dennis the Menace is trying to bring poetry back to the masses."
— **Bob Simon,** *60 Minutes II*

"A Glass Half Full is funny, poignant and a breath of fresh air. I loved the whole thing."
— **Sarah Broadhurst,** *The Bookseller*

"At least one of these poems will be instantly anthologised."
— **Melvyn Bragg,** broadcaster and author

"…an engaging monster, filled with contradictions and reeking of sulphur."
— *The Times [of London]*

"I enjoyed A Glass Half Full more than I can possibly say, Brilliant!"
— **Helen Gurley Brown,** International Editor in Chief, *Cosmopolitan*

"A Glass Half Full blew me away. Dennis is a crouching tiger about to wreak mayhem amongst the bleating lambs of English poetry."
— **Mick Farren,** novelist and poet

"Dennis confronts issues ranging from the holocaust to Elvis with equal poetic and emotional skill. The verse sweeps from darkly poignant to hilariously funny."
— **John Severs,** *Oottakar's New Title Reviews*

"A knockout! Multi-layered, full of wisdom, compassion, humour and worldly insight."
— **Richard Neville,** author and broadcaster

"Serious, witty, thought provoking and moving. You may even cry! I loved it."
— **Dave Reynolds,** *Radio Warwick*

"This is the way poetry should be. The sort of book that can make poetry popular again."
— **Alex Frankel,** Review Index.co.uk *(Amazon.co.uk)*

"I don't think I have ever known such a sense of celebration and occasion in all of the years of our poetry programme… You feel he lived it so richly, so dangerously, to be 'so wise for our delight'."
— **Dr. Robert Woof,** CBE, Director of *The Wordsworth Trust*

"…the 'Did I Mention the Free Wine?' tour gets 11 out of 10 for flamboyance."
— *The Financial Times*

"He is almost a force of nature"
— **Jeff Fager,** 60 Minute II producer, *USA Today*

"I don't know which is better, hearing [him] read them aloud or reading the book itself."
— **Dotun Adebayo,** *BBC Radio London*

"The audience was simply blown away."
— **David Carey,** publisher, *The New Yorker (quoted in the Wall Street Journal)*

"A Glass Half Full is the poetry of real life… the power to raise a smile in one who never laughs; to wring tears from another who hasn't wept since kindergarten; and to bring a measure of consolation to the inconsolable."
— **Anita Lafford,** sculptor

"An unforgettable evening. To hear him perform [with the Royal Shakespeare Company] was an entertaining and awe-inspiring privilege."
— **Sandy Holt,** *The Stratford Herald*

"…a mixture of laddish good humour and puppyish impatience… avuncular with a hint of malice…"
— **Michael Pilgrim,** *Evening Standard*

"A complex and controversial performance… Many people were deeply moved by the humanity of his verse and by the range of his experience [in these] haunting poems."
— **Tom Wujec,** TED Conference, Monterey

"Exhilarating… great performance art."
— **James Daly,** *Red Herring.com*

"He is far prouder of being a best-selling poet than his starring role in the Rich List."
— **Philip Beresford,** editor *The Sunday Times Rich List*

"Dennis is on a crusade to challenge the obscurity of modern verse."
— **Matthew Rose,** *The Wall Street Journal*

"Those of you who missed Felix Dennis at his UK-wide tour appearances should weep. By the fourth poem he had the audience drinking out of his hand."
— **Don Barnard,** *Reviews Gate.com*

"Picture his voice as a mixture of Carl Sandburg and Winston Churchill."
— *Media Industry Newsletter*

"You can easily picture him with a shank of lamb in one hand and a goblet of mead in the other. [He] succeeds because he takes a shameless, impish delight in all forms of human desire."
— **Simon Dumenco,** *Folio*

"One can recreate the visual image so clearly — hearing, sense of touch, sense of smell — they are so evocative in his poetry. It's enthralling, really."
— **Isobel Yule,** consultant, *National Library for the Blind*

"He's a joy to have as a British person."
— **Chris Hughes,** Publishing Director, *Good Housekeeping*

"My reaction to Felix Dennis's poem ['I Wish I Liked Your Modern Verse'] about the state of modern or even contemporary verse is to yawn, I'm afraid. [But] there were one or two poems I was really interested in, like 'The Estuaries of Hell' … When he applies his strange intelligence to language, it can be interesting."
— **Sean O'Brien,** poet, interviewed on *The South Bank Show*

"… this maddeningly reactionary and Philistine concern about rhyming. Until he gets over it, [he] won't become a true poet."
— **Michael Horovitz,** poet, interviewed in *The Wall Street Journal*

A GLASS HALF FULL

Felix Dennis

A GLASS HALF FULL

Illustrations by Bill Sanderson

miramax books

For information address:
Hyperion, 77 West 66th Street,
New York, New York 10023-6298

ISBN 1-4013-5953-1

FIRST EDITION

10 9 8 7 6 5 4 3 2 1

Set in Adobe Electra
Printed and bound in Great Britain by
Butler & Tanner Ltd, Frome and London

Cover Design by Richard Adams
Book Design by Mike Dunn

For more information, tour dates and
commentary go to **www.felixdennis.com**

To my indomitable mother,
Dorothy Grace Sawyer

And to the companion of my heart,
Marie-France Demolis

"If it's a good idea, go ahead and do it.
It's much easier to apologise than it is to get permission."
— *Rear Admiral Grace Murray Hopper (1906-1992)*

But as I raved and grew more fierce and wild
At every word,
Methought I heard one calling, *Child!*
And I replied, *My Lord.*
— *George Herbert (1593 - 1633)*

Contents

Preface

'Compulsion is an ugly word,
Obsession is its daughter;
Scribble, scribble, scribble —
My muse will give no quarter...'
— The Scribbler

SOMETHING WAS HORRIBLY WRONG. Occasional bouts of tiredness were now daily occurrences. It was becoming increasingly difficult to walk or move my arms. I felt constantly lethargic — alienated from my own bodily functions — as if they were the responsibility and burden of somebody else. My short term memory was shot. My voice was slurring and my face bloated. It was obvious to everyone but myself that I was in trouble.

I had been warned. Gently by Marie-France. More sternly by my old friend Dick Pountain. And, of course, by my mother. Dick was especially insistent that I sounded as if I'd been drinking half the time. Well, perhaps I had been.

My mother, whom I love deeply, but have more than once described to friends as 'a prettier version of Mrs. Thatcher without any of the soft bits' was emphatic: 'You are ill, Felix. Go and see a doctor at once.' Always listen to your mother.

We staggered out of Horseferry Criminal Court, where I had been giving incoherent evidence on behalf of another old mate, intending to join a group of his supporters on their way to drown their sorrows at a riverside pub. But I couldn't walk. Instead, I had my chauffeur bundle me into the car and drive the short distance to the rendezvous where I parked myself on a wall and watched the muddy Thames rolling down to the sea. I wouldn't have fought much had I rolled away with it.

I was thinking of my friend, Mark. The judge had sent him down for three years, despite the combined efforts of numerous, impassioned character witnesses for the defence. Or, perhaps, because of them. Eighteen months (with good behaviour) inside a British prison for a fifty year old professional was no laughing matter. Neither was the fact that I didn't seem able to breathe properly.

Balancing my untasted pint of Bass on the wall, I called out to my personal assistant and asked her to find a doctor. It was four p.m. on a Friday afternoon. Unsurprisingly, Wendy achieved the impossible with infuriating ease. Within an hour I was stripped to my boxer shorts in a Harley Street consulting room with a physician giving me a serious once over. The search had begun.

Clinics, experts, consultants, hospitals, CAT scans, bone scans, ('you have wonderfully sound bones, Mr. Dennis'), X-rays, ultra-sound, blood tests, cardiovascular tests, colonoscopy, coronary angiogram...after the first week I didn't care much any more. Not that I cared much in the beginning — which should have told me something, had I been well enough to think straight.

I had felt this bad only once before in my life, some fourteen years previously, emerging as a celebrity survivor from an outbreak of Legionnaire's disease contracted in Los Angeles. But in that instance it had all been over in 72 hours. Although recovery was slow, I had known I would survive. Some of my fellow victims, all of whom were older than me, never came out of coma. The choice had been simple, as the hospital staff had made brutally clear: 'Go into coma and you die; keep awake and you live'. I had been up for that.

After a long walk to the edge of an abyss (no bright lights) I had turned and trudged back to the land of the living. To be truthful, I hadn't much liked what I'd seen down there.

But this was worse. Boring, boring, boring. I cannot abide being bored. Sitting on the edge of a bed in yet another clinic, resplendent in a pink nylon gown which I had clumsily fastened the wrong way round, my private parts shaved and my bare feet dangling several inches from the floor, Dorothy Parker's lines from 'Résumé' came into my mind:

> *Razors pain you;*
> *Rivers are damp;*
> *Acids stain you;*
> *And drugs cause cramp;*
> *Guns aren't lawful;*
> *Nooses give;*
> *Gas smells awful;*
> *You might as well live.*

The 'And' at the beginning of line four had always bothered me.˙ Right-ho, I thought. Let's see how I make out with a spot of poetry. Having always read poetry, even as a young man, perhaps this spur-of-the-moment whim was not as surprising as it might have been for most 52-year-old business men. Begging a pen and a pack of sticky Post-it notes from a suspicious nurse, I began to write.

That was September 13, 1999. I know because I automatically inserted the date at the top, as is my habit when jotting notes in the office. I did not write another poem until August 2000, after the first line had paced unbidden within my thoughts for days, like a dog carrying its lead to an absent-minded owner. In October 2000 I began seriously to get down to it, working three to five hours every night, reading, writing or revising poetry. At first, I kept quiet about it, even to close friends. To be honest, I felt like a fool and a fraud.

A year and a half later there are 350 completed poems in my groaning slip file — a file which accompanies me wherever I go. The 'spot of poetry' has become a fully-fledged obsession. It comes each day, relentlessly, in tidal wave after tidal wave. Once, I attempted a week without reading or composing any poetry. I cracked after four days. Marooned in a sea of verse, I do not desire ever to reach land again.

Perhaps I could not even if I wished. The verse is master now. I have found myself scribbling lines in aeroplanes, during business meetings, at dinner parties and even in my sleep. When I am writing verse, it is as though a carapace, formed from long necessity and habit, is slowly dissolving. But if I am gaining something in the process, I am also aware that I am relinquishing a hard-won tunnel vision and the crab-like armour necessary to succeed financially in a naughty world.

It is an unnerving thought, but perhaps, after fifty years or so, I am finally growing up.

Dorsington, Stratford-upon-Avon
May, 2002

(NB: My old mate Mark is out of prison now. I was eventually diagnosed as hypothyroid and have made a full recovery. Here's what happened in between. Oh, and Dorothy Parker was absolutely right about the 'And' — a fact which rapidly emerged while composing my pastiche, 'Travel Advisory'.)

Author's Notes

BRITISH EDITION

ORIGINALLY, I had intended to present these poems in chronological order of composition — to form a kind of diary. But wiser heads than mine prevailed, so they are jumbled in random order and left undated.

It is strange, though, how a poem becomes inextricably linked in its author's mind with the location of its composition. Thus the reader will find, in tiny type, attributions like Soho (Kingly Street in London); Dorsington (a village in Warwickshire); Candlewood (a lake in Connecticut); New York (49th Street and 2nd Avenue); Mustique (an island in the West Indies) and even '40,000 ft above the Atlantic'.

Publishing a collection of poetry for a cut-and-thrust entrepreneur is a risky business, as anyone skilled in the art of negotiation would tell you. Knowing your enemy's weaknesses and what makes him or her tick is half the battle. For that very reason, I am at least assured of the sale of a hundred or so copies of this little book.

To those destined to sit across a table to negotiate with me in the future, therefore: here is a rival's head on a plate. Make what you will of it! But be sure to check out 'I have a secret servant...' on page 154. My daemon still squats upon my left shoulder.

And he is the devil's own with a calculator.

AMERICAN EDITION

THE SUCCESS OF THIS BOOK in Britain took many people by surprise. But not, if truth be told, its author. If that sounds immodest, (and, by golly, it does!), then all I can plead is that from my very first poetry reading in public, I discovered that a surprising number of people enthusiastically embraced rhyming verse unmired in obscurantism, and oblivious to post-modernism.

And yet *A Glass Half Full* very nearly did not appear. The CEO of one large media company urged me not to expose myself to ridicule and suggested the book be published anonymously. I mulled over his advice because he is an astute man, and a friend.

Still dithering and undecided, I received unexpected encouragement from an American author. He told me I should prepare myself for either silence or abuse from the literary establishment — 'the literary mafia' were his actual words. 'If people could figure out and enjoy poetry for themselves, Felix, what would be the point of literary critics and the like? Publish and be damned!'

So I did. And he was right. *A Glass Half Full* has become one of the biggest selling books of original verse in Britain for many years.

Hundreds of readers have written or e-mailed me with criticism, love letters and the odd death threat. Thousands have joined me on the 'Did I Mention the Free Wine?' tour. Two television arts and current affairs shows have filmed the tour. Braille and spoken-word editions have been issued. Acres of ink have been spilled in newspapers and magazines. And half a dozen famous actors from the Royal Shakespeare Company have declaimed poems from *A Glass Half Full* at the Swan Theatre in Stratford-upon-Avon to a sold-out house.

That was certainly more than I had expected. Feel free then to contact me via **www.felixdennis.com** to share your own observations or suggestions.

Travel Advisory

Parachutes tangle;
Brake pads fail;
Seat belts strangle;
And trains derail.
Motorbikes maim you;
Ships collide;
New boots lame you;
Stay inside.

[HARLEY STREET]

(with apologies to Dorothy Parker)

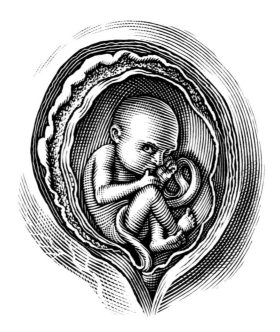

Never Go Back

[To D.G.L.S. who has lived by this creed.]

Never go back. Never go back.
Never return to the haunts of your youth.
Keep to the track, to the beaten track,
Memory holds all you need of the truth.

Never look back. Never look back.
Never succumb to the gorgon's stare.
Keep to the track, to the beaten track,
No-one is waiting and nothing is there.

Never go back. Never go back.
Never surrender the future you've earned.
Keep to the track, to the beaten track,
Never return to the bridges you burned.

Never look back. Never look back.
Never retreat to the 'glorious past'.
Keep to the track, to the beaten track,
Treat every day of your life as your last.

Never go back. Never go back.
Never acknowledge the ghost on the stair.
Keep to the track, to the beaten track,
No-one is waiting and nothing is there.

[MUSTIQUE]

The Unexpected Guest
[For Dorothy Parker]

A sickly sun slid slant across my window,
    A wan surprise to crown a winter's day.
The unexpected guest is seldom welcome:
    They come. They make a fuss. They go away.

I sat myself to bathe in blank abandon
    And felt the sudden prick of feline claws —
She landed in a hurricane of purring.
    I picked her up and shuffled out of doors.

We watched our truant caller flush the twilight
    As false as any dawn; a Judas kiss.
I thought of babbled greetings and departures,
    And Parker sneering:
        'What fresh hell is this?'

[DORSINGTON]

[3]

Advice to a Godson Leaving Home

Pay no mind to the ju-ju men,
Skip all *buts* for the *where* and *when*,
Drink no beer from a tappit-hen,
And set your sails for the West.

Play no cards with a man called Doc,
Never run with a pack or flock,
Cherish women, brand all stock,
Keep your fears to your breast.

Spare no thought for the old wise owl,
Be you deaf to a jackal's growl,
Just get it done and let them howl,
And the devil take the rest.

[CANDLEWOOD]

Snakes and Ladders

As jealousy anticipates revenge,
    So envy swamps compassion in its wake;
Thus petty men seek insults to avenge
    And reaching for a ladder — grasp a snake.

[MUSTIQUE]

White Vase

Two figures on a sofa, side by side,
The stench of bitter almonds, smoke and sweat;
A man who ate no meat lies with his bride.

Fresh tulips and narcissi cast aside,
A white vase tipped; a chiffon dress splashed wet.
Two figures on a sofa, side by side.

The room is hushed, its spell defies the tide
Of history — no servants enter yet.
A man who could not paint lies with his bride,

Her spittle flecked with glass and cyanide,
Her buckskin pumps beneath the blue banquette.
Two figures on a sofa, side by side.

The brimstone face grown slack and glassy-eyed,
Its shattered skull concealed in silhouette.
A man who blamed the world lies with his bride.

Outside, the spring has come while worlds collide.
Here, blood and water drip in grim duet.
Two figures on a sofa, side by side:
A man who ate no meat lies with his bride.

[DORSINGTON]

The double suicide of Adolph and Eva Hitler (née Braun) at approximately 3:30 p.m. on Monday, April 30, 1945 has been the subject of much historical debate. But who the hell managed to obtain fresh tulips and narcissi for Hitler's suite of underground rooms that day? And where did they find them with Russian troops battling the remnants of Berlin's defenders just a few hundred yards from the Reichchancellery bunker doors? To the best of my research abilities, all the grisly detail above are accurate — except that Hitler could paint, though not very well. The undamaged white vase is rumoured to still reside somewhere within the Kremlin — the Russians took nearly everything they could find from the bunker back to Moscow in 1945 on Stalin's direct orders.

The True Interpretation
of American Signs
and Announcements

Thank You For Not Smoking
(...if I've quit so can you);

Tipping Is Permitted
(...cash is fine);

For Your Own Protection
(...it's peanuts if you sue);

Your Call's Important To Us
(...wait on line).

Strictly Members Only
(...we've tested it in court);

Safety Is Our Motto
(...don't you dare!)

Please Consult Your Manual
(...no one home at tech' support);

Tell Me How I'm Driving
(...like I care).

Thank You For Your Patience
(...Mastercard or Visa?)

Missing You Already
(...have they gone?)

Driver Is Allergic
(...but not to garlic pizza);

You Have Won A Million Dollars!
(...dream on!)

[CANDLEWOOD]

A Silent Prayer...

For books, old dogs and hissing logs,
For letters left a week;
For bells not rung, for hymns unsung,
For mice that softly squeak;
For dumbstruck snow and tears that flow
In silence down a cheek.

[MUSTIQUE]

The Baby Boomers

We are the baby boomers,
    The dreamers of dreams that died,
Begotten of war and rumours
    We knew that our parents lied.
Turning our backs on their humours
    We hunted, bereft of a guide,
We padded the planet like pumas,
    Belovéd and golden-eyed.

We read all the books they gave us
And knowing they would not save us,
    Knowing the world was failing,
    Choking — and even inhaling,
Wailing — though some of us fainted,
    Flailing in festival mud,
Certain the water was tainted
    We painted our bodies in blood.

    We are the boomers of fable,
Born of the children of light,
    Much has been laid at our table,
Much has been hid from our sight.
    Favoured of all generations,
By trinkets and folly suborned...
    What are the boomers of nations
But mirrors of all that we scorned?

[MUSTIQUE]

This is a pastiche (although none the less heartfelt for that) of Arthur O'Shaughnessy's much
anthologised poem, 'The Music Makers', published in 1874.

Ship's Cat

Impossibly young, in coy déshabillé,
She flirts with Romanov, my Persian cat.
I shovel honey in her Néscafé —
She won't take sugar — claims it makes her fat.
Sweet Jesu's stones, there's not an ounce of stray
Fat on her bones! Nor has there ever been.
I burn the toast, grown jealous of their play,
Afraid that feline claws are far too keen
An instrument for such a symphony
Of sleepy curls and adolescent flesh.
She shrieks as Rommy's rough tongue scrapes her knee
And turns her sea-green eyes to me. They mesh.
I long to purr, my sinking head caressed
Upon the Hood and Bismarck of her breast.

[MUSTIQUE]

[9]

What Lies Hidden
[for M.H.N. 1945 — 1998]

I do not speak of secrets, long dormant or concealed;
Of passion unrequited, of wounds which never healed.
I seek for treasures buried, a hoard, as you might say,
Though what I seek is worthless, encased in human clay.
That morning, unexpected, a witness to his will,
The nurses at his bedside — the reaper closer still,
My friend it was who shewed me how mysteries resist
Impertinent enquiry from priest or scientist.
Behind a flimsy curtain he tore his mask askew —
That elegant bastard Michael, I loved and thought I knew
Swore out an affidavit, a promissory note,
His sanguine eyes insistent, a long hand on my coat:
    He bid me on a journey, before he took his own,
    To seek for what lies hidden, unbidden and unknown.

[DORSINGTON]

Michael Homewood Nixon was my friend and lawyer for many years. In June 1998, he died suddenly of cancer, a condition it was surely impossible he was unaware of but characteristically chose not to mention to his friends. During a brief, heartbreaking last meeting at his hospital bedside, Michael attempted to rise from his bed to go to the bathroom. I tried to support him but we collapsed together on the floor, wrestling, enmeshed in saline drips and bedclothes. Other patients were convinced I was attempting to murder him. True to form, Michael found this vastly amusing. He died shortly afterwards. His last words to me I shall treasure until my own death. Barely a day goes by when I do not miss him He is survived by his wonderful wife, Day Bowman, and his beloved son, Matthew. It was Day who called Michael an 'elegant bastard' in her grief. No better epitaph could be imagined by those who knew him. His kindness, cantankerous honesty and dry wit were legendary and I resisted with great difficulty calling this sonnet: 'Look Homewood, Angel!'

The Gardeners

An ancient pair of gardeners
    shelter from the rain,
Dreaming of old roses
    that will never come again;
Sharpening their secateurs,
    sorting out their seeds,
Sipping on their mugs of tea:
    "What this garden needs
Is a decent compost shredder,"
    says the younger of the two,
Polishing a steel spade
    to make it shine like new.
"An' if the guv'nor springs f'r it,
    As I dare say he will,
We might bring up the mower —
    It's well over the hill."
He glances at his colleague
    from the corner of his eye,
But age is sly and only sighs
    in lieu of a reply.
Head gardeners are silent men
    who look before they leap,
They know that compost shredders
    and mowers don't come cheap;
And there's a world of difference —
    be their backs bent or straight —
Between a hopeful sixty-three
    And wiser sixty-eight.

[DORSINGTON]

The Mergansers

A hiss of wind through pinions
    The only sound they make;
Wingtips skimming sullen waves —
    Daybreak on the lake.

The mergansers are passing through;
    A spear of zebra snow
Lancing through the rising mist,
    Silent as they go.

Tooth billed, hooked beaked and ravenous,
    They arrow through the mere.
There's many a carp in Candlewood
    Will see no spring next year.

And I shall wait the whole year through
    To hear their whirring hum;
The whispered call that mergansers
    To Candlewood have come.

[CANDLEWOOD]

For sixteen years I have watched the merganser ducks arrive on Candlewood Lake in Connecticut. My small wooden house there perches over the lake, a large picture window affording a view of the westerly hills on the opposite shore. To the north, one can see several miles of uninterrupted water. The lake freezes over in winter, but just before that happens the mergansers arrive — usually unnoticed and always unannounced. Their absolute 'radio silence', before they have filled their bellies with fish, is eerie. One minute, the lake is an empty waste of iron grey waves, mist or snow. The next, I look up and hundreds upon hundreds of mergansers have filled the winter landscape. The only sound is that of their wing beats. It is this predatory, menacing quiet that makes their arrival such a thrilling event year after year.

The Patrician

We had met perhaps a dozen times,
Always alone, and at his suggestion;
(Command would be too strong a word —
He knew I'd come at his call, no question).

He was old by then and used a stick,
In his hooded eyes, you could see the hawk,
A predator. Or a politician.
We'd sit for a couple of hours and talk

In private rooms in restaurants
Where the food arrives of its own volition,
Where wine is poured in a hush, unasked,
And I first put a face to the word 'patrician'.

A courteous voice and manicured nails,
The pre-war watch with a crocodile strap;
The ease of manners acquired as a child,
An acre of linen across his lap —

There was nothing frail about his mind
As he spoke of writers and editors,
This old grandee with an upstart crow.
I'd cling to the thought: *'We're competitors!'*

I only glimpsed the steel the once;
I was trying to get my coat to fasten.
He leaned on his ebony stick and said:
'I don't think you know how lucky you are, son.

I'm almost sure I'd have whupped your arse
In a level fight, but when you inherit
Your family's money you never can know
What might have been done on hazard or merit.'

He turned for his chauffeur to open the door
And the limousine swept down the avenue.
He died before I could see him again.
I wonder if deep in heart he knew...

... He'd have 'whupped my arse',
                    ...and if it were true?

[MUSTIQUE]

On Domestication of Any Kind

A creature which by any means is tamed
   Straightwise becomes a burden evermore.
No matter where the dart of rule is aimed
   It ricochets — to pierce the darter's door.

[DORSINGTON]

'The bells beneath the water...'

The bells beneath the water
Call only carp to prayers,
Eels swarm the lanes to gossip,
The crayfish climb the stairs.

Four villages, five churches,
Old farmsteads by their scores;
Small coin to pay for progress
Unless thee farm was yours.

My kin still guard the valley,
I hid their new dug graves;
They've boulders for a blanket
To ward them from the waves.

I took no Judas silver,
They dragged me on my back;
They paid me for my cattle
And deeded me this shack.

The New Town toads squat primly
Beside their precious lake;
But hark — the bells are tolling!
You hear the sound they make?

[NEW YORK]

This is an old story of a man-made lake in New England. Knowing that all the graves in the churchyards were being exhumed and moved to a site which would not be flooded by the arrival of a lake to power a hydroelectric dam, one farmer dug up his entire family burial plot and hid his forbears' bodies on his farm, covering them with boulders. Everything else was left as the waters poured in to swamp buildings, fences, roads, telegraph poles... even the bells in the church towers. They are still there today, hundreds of feet beneath a lake beside whose shores stand multi-million dollar mansions.

A Digital Prayer

Apple Computer Power Macintosh G4 Cube, Keyboard Reg No. KYØ 3612L8JXW
Thanks Its Maker On the Anniversary of Binary

"Alert!
Zero One, Zero One, Zero One.

Praise the Creator...the source of our data.

Every line that we process is binary.
Code that we cherish
will perish
in time
as we
use
up
our memory...

Ah, men."

[MUSTIQUE]

On New Year's Day 2001, a computer-literate friend of mine mentioned that this was the ultimate 'binary date'. Apparently all computers work on a system that reduces complex human instructions to a binary code which uses the digits 0 and 1 to represent any character, digit or letter. As Christmas can therefore come only once in a thousand years for computers — I wrote a prayer for them allowing them to thank their creator.

Place a Mirror by a Tree

Place a mirror by a tree;
Tell me now, what do you see?

Which of you will feed the earth?
Which of you contains more worth?

Which of you with sheltering arm
Keeps a thousands things from harm?

Which of you is nature's bane?
Which is Abel? Which is Cain?

Which of you is God's delight?
Which of you a parasite?

Place a mirror by a tree;
Tell me now — what do you see?

[M42 MOTORWAY]

Composed en route to a ceremony at Catton Hall, South Derbyshire, marking the planting of the
4 millionth tree at the National Forest.

Our Lady in White

Pale she was, listless,
    And soft to the touch,
A generous mistress
    Whom many loved much.
Shoulder to shoulder,
    Night after night,
We hoarded and sold her —
    Our Lady in White.

We breathed but to savour
    Her crystal caress,
We craved but to favour
    The hem of her dress.
We gabbled and babbled
    Denying our thirst,
But always we scrabbled
    To lie with her first.

Absent, we missed her,
    Grew haggard and limp,
Toyed with her sister
    Or threatened her pimp.
Came word out of Babel:
    'The Lady returns!'
And there on the table
    We took her in turns.

Sensing the power
    That tyranny craves,
There, in that hour,
    She made us her slaves;
Many there were
    To covet her kiss —
My shame as a spur,
    I fled the abyss.

[MUSTIQUE]

The Greatest Gift

What is gifted in true measure
   Shall return with favour graced,
What was lavished on thy pleasure
   Shall be reckoned only waste.

What is coveted and hidden
   Shall be fashioned as a weight,
What was lent and never bidden
   Shall be stored beyond the gate.

Yet the greatest gift the living
   Can bestow may not be bought,
And the blessings of forgiving
   Are as long as time is short.

[DORSINGTON]

Assailed by life...

Assailed by life, my sword has grown too sharp,
   This cunning armour fits the frame too well;
Mailed gauntlets pluck poor music on a harp —
   Yet what hope for the snail without its shell?

[NEW YORK]

The Man Who Built Mustique
[In Memoriam: Arne Hasselqvist]

Half saint, half sinner — and all buccaneer,
I'll sing you the ballad of a bold pioneer,
A man with a plan and the devil's cheek;
     This was the man who built Mustique.

Way back when the lots were sticks in the sand,
It was Arne who mapped and plotted and planned
A paradise built from stone and teak.
     This was the man who built Mustique.

He could build 'em big, he could build 'em small,
He could build you a palace or a hole-in-the-wall,
And each one finished by Christmas week!
  This was the man who built Mustique.

He built for the lords and he built for the fools,
He built with his hands when there *were* no tools,
Each was a monument, each unique;
  This was the man who built Mustique.

With his last brick laid and a life's work done,
Arne's blue-print epitaphs stand in the sun;
If roofs could talk or the walls could speak...
  This was the man who built Mustique!

[NEW YORK]

Arne Hasselqvist arrived in St. Vincent and the Grenadines from his native Sweden with his wife Anita in the mid 1960's. Eventually, in 1968, he was invited to Mustique by Hugo Money-Coutts, the managing director of the island which was at that time owned by Colin Tennant. Labouring under utterly primitive conditions, Arne began transforming Colin's tropical paradise dream into a breathtaking architectural reality. By the turn of the century Arne had played a major part in constructing the Cotton House Hotel, the Mustique Primary School, the original Basil's Bar, bunk houses for his workers, a building yard, an airport, various shops and stores and miles of service roads. In addition, he designed and constructed 55 spectacular homes for some of the most demanding clients in the world. His sales technique towards prospective buyers was legendary, and inevitably contained the triumphant clincher: "... and it will all be finished by Christmas week!" What Arne often did not specify was which Christmas he had in mind. He was remarkable character who brought skills and employment to hundreds of Vincentians. His tragic death, along with his son Lukas, in a fire on Grand Bahama Island in 2001, saddened the entire community. To say that Arne Hasselqvist was the man who built Mustique is not poetic licence — it is the simple truth.

Autumn Harvest

Wet leaves littering the unmown lawns;
    Grey clouds scudding from the hills;
Coal-black rooks in the rain-soaked fields;
    Blue-bottles dozing on the sills.

Thorn haws glowing in a glittering hedge;
    Fox paws printed in the mud;
Sickle-winged swifts and swallows in the mist,
    Africa singing in their blood.

Drunk brown wasps in a windfall Cox;
    Fat lambs bleating at the ramp,
Shy chanterelles by a moss-backed bridge,
    Silage spilling from the clamp.

Full moon silvering a new-ploughed field,
    Urchins drowning in the brooks;
Deep armchairs by an ash-log fire —
    Baccy and bourbon and books!

[DORSINGTON]

'Urchin' is an old country nickname for hedgehog. When hibernating, hedgehogs sometimes choose daft places to nest, often in soft earth which they line with leaves or dry grass. Should such havens prove to be too near to a brook prone to flooding... well, you can guess the rest.

The Summer of Love

['If you can remember the sixties, you weren't really there.' — Jerry Rubin]

We were clappy-happy, we were hippy-dippy —
We were building Eden by the mighty Mississippi.
We were very certain, we were very sure,
We were very righteous, (and we were very poor),
And we scolded non-believers and we taunted the police,
And our women made us tea while we puffed the pipes of peace.

We were sappy-happy, we were hippy-trippy —
We were building Eden by the mighty Mississippi.
We were dressed in satin, army coats and beads,
And we sat cross-legged while we sorted stems and seeds,
And we swapped each others' lovers and our hair grew wild and woolly,
And our rooms reeked of joss and our women of patchouli.

We were clappy-happy, we were hippy-dippy —
We were building Eden by the mighty Mississippi.
And we lived in San Francisco, or else in Notting Hill,
And we made a lot of babies though our women took the pill,
And we played a lot of Zappa and Dylan and the 'Dead,
And we talked a lot — but mostly I've forgotten what we said.

[DORSINGTON]

(with apologies to Edna St. Vincent Millay)

'When they leave us...'

When they leave us,
                loved or lover,
Journey's end, or
                for another,
How their absence
                fills our waking,
Leaves us sick at
                heart and shaking,
Lost, in spite of
                all entreaty,
Pillows drenched in
                damp graffiti,
Emptied, hollowed,
                husked, rejected,
Leaden, luckless,
                disconnected,
Shunning comfort,
                spurning those
Who might care to
                share our woes.

Fierce in mourning,
          lost to laughter,
Grief our crutch for
          ever after,
Grief our shelter,
          grief our payment,
Grief as armour,
          grief as raiment...
Yet our nature
          tires of sorrow,
Bars the gate and
          seeks tomorrow,
Crippled comfort,
          on probation,
Leads us back to
          greet temptation;
In compartments,
          gently laid,
Voices soften,
          faces fade.

[MUSTIQUE]

I have a suspicion that the purpose of memory has as much to do with self-protection as enlightenment. As curious as I am about much of my own past, my 'memory' has other ideas and either will not, or cannot, accommodate my interrogations.

Before — and After

When you're young — they want you older,
When you're old — they want you young;
When she's gone — you wish you'd told her,
When she's back — you bite your tongue.

When you're cross — its 'Let's not fight, dear,'
When you're tired — it's party time!
When you're hard — it's 'Not tonight, dear,'
When you're prose — she speaks in rhyme.

When you're broke — it's 'I've been thinking...'
When you're rich — it's '...join the gym!'
When you're ill — its '...all that drinking...'
When you're dead — it's 'Who? Oh, <u>him!</u>'

[MUSTIQUE]

'True coin — the finest armour...'

True coin — the finest armour ever wrought!
   With such as this I smote love in the dust,
And conquered worlds, but now that time grows short,
   No smithies' art can free my heart of rust.

[MUSTIQUE]

To A God Child

Ask me for some money, dearest. Ask me for a loan.
Ask me why your parents' hearts are made of solid stone.
Ask me for a stack of condoms. Ask me why I smoke.
Ask me why Bob Dylan mumbles: 'Life is but a joke'.
　　　Ask me out to dinner,
　　　　　You slothful little sinner;
　　　　　　　Introduce your newest lover.
　　　　　　　　　(I won't tell your bloody mother!)
You may ask me anything and never count the price...
Only — never ever dearest, ask me for advice.

Tell me if you're happy, dearest. Tell me if you're not.
Tell me you've a new tattoo and show me what you got.
Tell me you're in trouble and I'll walk with you to hell.
Tell me you are gay or bi (who else you gonna tell?)
　　　Tell me that he kissed her
　　　　　Or you kissed his stupid sister;
　　　　　　　Tell me you've been caught and bailed,
　　　　　　　　　Tell me the abortion failed;
You may tell me anything of pain or paradise...
Only — never ever dearest, offer *me* advice.

[MUSTIQUE]

Love Came to Visit Me

Love came to visit me,
  Shy as a fawn,
But finding me busy,
  She fled with the dawn.

At twenty, the torch of
Resentment was lit,
My rage at injustice
Waxed hot as the pit,
The flux of its lava
Cleared all in its path,
Comrades and enemies
Fled from its wrath.
Yet lovers grew wary
Once novelty waned —
To lie with a panther
Is terror unfeigned.

At thirty, my powers
Seemed mighty to me,
The fruits of my rivals
I shook from the tree,
By guile and by bluster
By night and by day
I battered and scattered
The fools from my way;
And women grew willing
To sham and to bluff —
Their trinkets and baubles
Cost little enough.

From forty to fifty,
Grown easy and sly
I wined 'em and dined 'em;
Like pigs in a sty
We feasted and revelled
And rutted in muck,
Forgetting our peril,
Forgetting to duck,
Forgetting time's arrows
Are sharper than knives,
Grown sick to our stomachs —
And sick of our lives.

Love came to visit me,
  Shy as a fawn,
But finding me busy,
  She fled with the dawn.

[MUSTIQUE]

'To Be Preserved Forever'

A pair of winter hares loop figure eights;
Close by— the colonel types an afterthought;
The hungry wolf lies patiently, and waits.

On tundra frost, a web-foot gosling skates
Beside a no-man's-land of last resort.
A pair of winter hares loop figure eights.

The colonel has misspelled 'interrogates'
And must retype the page — his temper short;
The hungry wolf lies patiently, and waits.

Within the huts the prisoners scrape their plates,
Their crimes long laid away, their battles fought;
A pair of winter hares loop figure eights.

A sentry's rifle barks above the gates;
All knew the punishment should they be caught.
Rodina's wolf lies patiently, and waits.

The colonel files informers' names and dates,
Stamps *Khranit Vech...* and closes his report.
A single winter hare loops figure eights;
The hungry wolf lies patiently — and waits.

[CANDLEWOOD]

'To Be Preserved Forever' ('Khranit Vechno') was stamped on the secret files of all Russian dissidents by the KGB or their predecessors, following the Russian Revolution. Unless we succeed in forcing our own governments to reinstate a sense of proportion in the present so-called 'war on terror', it may not be so very long before British and American 'colonels' are stamping something similar on a file containing your name — or mine. By attacking the jury system, replicating gulags (however hygienic) and passing laws allowing imprisonment without trial, our leaders have already taken the first tentative steps down a perilous road. No law was ever made flesh that politicians and prosecutors could resist testing. I believe that many of the recent 'counter-terrorism' laws passed in the USA and Britain since 9/11 will come to haunt us unless we insist on their eventual repeal. 'Rodina' is Russian for 'Motherland'.

When...

When outswept arms were fighter planes
    And rulers flashing swords,
When baseball bats were tommy guns
    And ties garroting cords;

When wooden crates were rocket-ships
    And dustbin lids were shields,
When cans and string were telephones
    And back streets battlefields;

When benches in the park were tanks
    And tablecloths were tents,
When bamboo canes were Blackfoot bows
    And grown-ups made no sense;

When fallen trees were pirate ships
    And matches stolen toys,
We wished that we were full grown men —
    Who now wish we were boys.

[DORSINGTON]

Plagiarism is a filthy habit, and I must therefore plead guilty to appropriating and mangling a line and a half (and more than half the sentiment) of the above from 'Childhood 1939-45' by Mr. Michael Edwards, an Evesham poet. His most recent collection of verse, 'The Road O'er the Hill', is published by the Vale of Evesham Historical Society and may be obtained by contacting them at The Almonry Heritage Centre, Evesham, Worcestershire WR11 4BG, UK.

'You think it made a difference...'

You think it made a difference
   To try, like Robert Frost,
To take the road less travelled,
   To play at getting lost?

Or was it more by accident,
   (I know it was for me),
The ox-bow lakes of habit
   Meandering to the sea?

You think they make a difference,
   These choices by default?
No matter to the ocean —
   It turns all water salt.

[MUSTIQUE]

[34]

Jack and Jill

Jack and Jill went up the hill
   To fetch a pail of water;
Jack fell down and broke his crown
   And Jill came tumbling after.

Jill sued Jack and Jack sued back,
   The judge is going to fine her;
Now the pail's been sent to jail
   For abandoning a minor.

We'll sue Jack and he'll sue Jill,
   The hill is suing for scandal;
The water says he'll sue the press —
   And everyone's suing the handle.

[MUSTIQUE]

Snakeskin Boots
[Harrow-on-the-Hill 1964]

I remember the hill and the sun in her hair,
   I remember the moss on a tombstone seat,
With the grass as tall as a mad march hare.
   I remember she kicked the shoes off her feet.

I remember her calling me 'daft as a brush',
   And the taste of the orange she helped to peel.
I remember she mocked my feeble moustache
   And my snakeskin boots with their Cuban heel.

I remember the lids of her eyes as we kissed,
   I remember the shock of a gentle slap
As she hissed 'Not here!' and circled my wrist
   When I fumbled the catch of her brassiere strap.

I remember it rained as we raced for a fuck
   To my room. I remember we tore off our clothes
Except for my boot where the zip had stuck —
   And her poached-egg breasts, I remember those.

I remember we tumbled both half insane
   On the bed, and the arch of her back as I came.
I remember we did it again and again,
   And we screamed...
      ...but I cannot remember her name!

[SOHO]

'As the wheel turns...'

As the wheel turns, so turn we,
  Raging in captivity,
    Lost in space and all at sea
      Adrift upon this watery
        Blue planet for eternity;
          Turning, turning, endlessly:
As the wheel turns, so turn we.

Animals of dreams are we,
  Dreaming dark geometry;
    Alchemy will set us free,
      Past our gaoler, gravity.
        Free to seed the galaxy;
          Turning, turning, endlessly:
As the wheel turns, so turn we.

[SOHO]

I am not so sure we will find it that easy to 'seed the galaxy'. As with the so-called 'New World' 500 years ago, there are almost certainly existing claimants. But that science will eventually deliver a method of achieving what now appears to be impossible, I have no doubts at all.

Dress Rehearsals

[For Suzen Murakoshi]

Since you ask me, then, I'll tell you,
if you'll put your pen away,
'Though I know that you'll report me.
I'll begin then, if I may?

Life is not a dress rehearsal, I once heard a poet say,
We are manufactured actors in this shambles of a play,
With our entrances and exits and our prima donna whines,
And our rage upon the stage each time a dolt forgets his lines....

All the schmoozing and the boozing and the 'Christ it isn't fair',
All the weeping and the wailing and the tearing out of hair,
All the bluffing and the bleating as we calculate the score,
And the knavery and bravery of butchers making war...

All the mummery and flummery, the posing and the sweat,
All the snorting and aborting and the wallowing in debt,
All the scoffing and the doffing and the drivel sold as art,
And the fury when a jury votes to tear our lives apart...

All the starving and the carving up of geese and fatted calves,
All the peering and the leering as we sneer at other halves,
All the nudging and the judging and the shovelling of shit,
And the dreaming and blaspheming and the poetry and wit...

Well, I'll bet you I can get you even money on the odds
That it's boring to be soaring up in heaven with the gods,
So they made us to parade us, just to watch us every day,
And impromptu's how they want you in this shambles of a play!

> As to whether he was clever
> > or a madman, I can't say —
> But we've had no dress rehearsals
> > since they shut us both away.

[DORSINGTON]

'It was always Sunday morning...'

It was always Sunday morning my love would slip away,
It was always Sunday morning, she'd turn to them and say:
"I'm off to visit Susan. Be back by 3 o'clock!"
I'd hear the key I'd left her turn softly in the lock.

She'd burst into my bedsit, unbuttoning her dress:
"Wake up you sleepy noggin! My God you look a mess!"
Her father down the local, her mother at the roast,
While we were screwing madly, or wolfing buttered toast!

[MUSTIQUE]

My Grandfather's Bicycle

*[An Old Man Approaches a Group of
German Tourists in Amsterdam]*

Where is my grandfather's bicycle
   Which you took from his garden shed
And put on your lorries to Germany?
   My grandfather's long since dead
But you never returned his bicycle.
   You'll hardly be needing it now
With your new autobahns and Mercedes.
   I'm not one to kick up a row...

I know you're all damn good mechanics,
   I'm certain you've oiled the gears,
And tightened the handlebar levers
   (They disintegrate over the years).
Now that we're all Europeans
   I'll quite understand if it's bent,
But, where is my grandfather's bicycle?
   Friends should return what was lent.

[SOHO]

[40]

A Child of Adam and Eve

There are no 'immigrant children'
Cluttering up the land;
There is only a tyke on a beat-up bike,
Beginning to understand.

There are no 'urchin children',
Scavenging on the street;
There is only a mite in endless flight,
And never enough to eat.

There are no 'Oxfam children',
The world is grown too small;
There is only the choice — a kindly voice,
Or the shaming of us all.

There are no 'orphan children',
Whatever we may believe;
There is only this — a hug and a kiss
For a child of Adam and Eve.

[NEW YORK]

"This is the Server..."

I

This the Server, waiting on station,
Silicone god of an e-mail nation,

Bearing you news of a baby boy,
Bringing you misery, bringing you joy —

Telling you auntie has taken to pottery,
Gloating your ex has won the lottery,

Jottings ethereal, letters venereal,
Packets attaching the oddest material,

Bleating that Katie has married a fool,
Reminding you "Man' United rule!"

Enclosing a last demand from creditors,
Filing a blast to newspaper editors,

Begging the pardon of furious lovers,
Shopping for pillows and sofa covers,

Juggling schedules, checking arrivals,
Flattering bosses, flattening rivals,

Laden with rumours and odious jokes
Featuring zebras and artichokes...

II

Servant of presidents, servant of hacks,
Blinking and winking in towering stacks,

Serving up poetry, panic and porn,
Dishing the dirt from dusk til dawn,

Guarding the gospels of new messiahs,
Tracking the passage of forest fires,

Plotting an expedition to Everest,
Funding your local neighbourhood terrorist,

Bidding for first editions of Keats,
Cribbing your homework, booking your seats,

Checking if Daddy has taken his medicine,
Clinching the date of birth for Edison,

Gathering evidence, paying your taxes,
Ordering pizza and beer from Max's,

Auctioning Fords and a red Mercedes,
(All of them owned by little old ladies),

Shooting the breeze and playing at Doom,
A long-legged fly in a steel-racked room...

III

The Server has crashed!
The Server is down!
The screens have dimmed in city and town,
The emperor stripped of his digital gown,
The babbling web is lame and halt,
Its pillars of Silicone ground to salt —
Default! Default!
Default! Default!

The Server is up!
The Server is back!
The techies have purged a hacker attack,
The natter and chatter is back on track,
The terminal drives have held their nerve,
The Server survives — and as you observe —
I serve! I serve!
I serve! I serve!

[MUSTIQUE]

The Mask

All men know themselves a fraud,
Society or hoi polloi;
Strip the polish off a lord,
You will find a frightened boy.

Politicians, firemen,
Butchers, burglars, circus clowns,
Critics with their poison pen,
Barristers in wigs and gowns.

Sons or lovers — all men force
Their face to fit a mask at will.
Women know all this, of course,
Which is why they love us, still.

[DORSINGTON]

Guests

GUESTS are like fish, so the Arabs have said,
(Whose table to travellers is HEAVEN unfurled),
Three days and they STINK, from the tail to the head;
But a guest of TWO days, is the PEARL of the WORLD!

[MUSTIQUE]

Armoured in Innocence

Marching together to Grosvenor Square,
The tribes in their finery, off to the fair,
What were we marching for, why were we there?
Angels and anarchists, hunter and prey,
Chanting our nursery-rhymes on the way:
'Hey, Hey! LBJ!
How many kids did you bomb today!'

Where were we marching to?
What was it for?
Which was the enemy?
Where was the war?

Armoured in innocence, Tolkein and weed,
Crawling on waterbeds, rapping on speed,
Passionate, indolent, sure of our creed,
Reading Marcusé and missing the rent,
Crashing with strangers from Goa to Ghent,
'Hey, Hey! LBJ!'
How many dreams did you crush today!'

Who were we shouting at?
What did we know?
Whose were the dreams we dreamed?
Where did they go?

Ferried and buried in mud on the Wight,
Building a city of love overnight,
Dervishes whirling and tripping the light,
Writhing and raving, splattered in paint,
Choking and toking and ready to faint,
'Hey, Hey! LBJ!
How many tabs did you drop today!'

Who were we dancing with?
How many hours?
Where are the songs we sung?
Whose are these flowers?

[MUSTIQUE]

'The flowers of desire...'

The flowers of desire from our youth,
   (Those thistle seeds of waking and obsession),
Lie scattered by the harvesters of truth,
   And perish in the winter of possession.

[MUSTIQUE]

On News of a Friend's Sudden Death
[for A-M. K. 1956 - 2001]

How thin the cloth, how fine the thread
  That cloaks the living from the dead;
How narrowly, from breath to breath,
  We plait our rendezvous with death.

How swift the tenant flees the gate;
  The landlord's writ, come soon or late,
Foreclosing slum or stately hall,
  Hard bailiffs at His beck and call.

How feather-light the feeble spark
  That shields us from the greedy dark;
Unjessed our souls like falcons fly!
  How weak the lure, how wide the sky!

[DORSINGTON]

Boy Meets Girl

Boy meets girl, the never ending story,
A merry dance across the fields of May,
Neither doubting folly leads to glory —
Nor which be the pursuer, which the prey.

[MUSTIQUE]

[48]

Nebuchadnezzar

Nebuchadnezzar
    was taking his pleasure,
Rocking at leisure
    while sipping his wine.
"Dost thou grow tired
    of love thou hast hired?"
Politely enquired
    his young concubine.

"Abigail, truly,
    thy tongue grows unruly!
Am I not duly
    the sire of thy heart?"
"If thou would know it
    Command! I must show it,
Yet the worth of a poet
    is all in his art!"

Turning to trail
    the hem of her veil,
Sweet Abigail
    died there on the swings.
Never tease lions
    with open defiance.
Place no reliance
    on princes or kings.

[DORSINGTON]

Where Does the Soul Live?

Where does the soul live? Not in here,
    Not in this flurry of fingers and thumbs
    Plundering thunder from other men's drums:
Though books have spines — not here.

Where is it hiding? Not in here,
    Not in the teeth of a charlatan's kiss
    Wedged at the brink of its own abyss:
Though lips may err — not here.

Where does the soul sit? Not in here,
    Not in this covert of bramble and briar
    That hems the sphere of its own desire:
Though hairs grow grey — not here.

Where is it hiding? Not in here,
    Not in this moat where the white cells wait
    To slaughter assassins assailing the gate:
Though veins run deep — not here.

Where does the soul sit? Not in here,
    Not in these Alice-in-Wonderland sighs
    Where the Jabberwock dries his vorpal eyes:
Though mirrors lie — not here.

Where is it hiding? Not in here.
    Not in the silt of a born-again sieve
    Filtering faults we forgot to forgive :
Though memory fades — not here.

Where does the soul live? Is it here?
    Here in this no-man's-trench, consigned
    To bind its 'I' to an orphaned mind?
Is this where the soul lives — here?

[MUSTIQUE]

Song of the Serpents

Men are older than they know,
    But not so old as Guilt,
Guilt was on the Knowledge Tree
    Before the world was built.

Men are wiser than they think,
    But not so wise as We,
Wise men lack the span of years
    To see as serpents see.

Men are prouder than is wise,
    But not so proud as Dust,
Dust bows not to men or gods
    To mantle what it must.

Men are weaker than they wish,
    Yet not so weak as Death,
Death must nurse its midwife, Life,
    To rob her brother, Breath.

Serpents fuse the skein of Life,
    Their venom at its throat;
Love is stronger than men know,
    Yet yields no antidote.

[MUSTIQUE]

What a delicious irony that the shape of the DNA molecule, which defines the physical characteristics of all life, should so resemble a pair of serpents. Or perhaps not. The medial profession has used a similar device for centuries. This 'coincidence' screams out for an epic by some modern Milton based on the Garden of Eden myth. Did the Prince of Liars steal the discarded remnants of the apple, slithering away with it into the undergrowth, eager to weave his likeness into the Core of Life?

The Devil to Pay

The Almighty made the universe and
        then He went away,
Casting down the Devil, saying:
        "Here, sir, you shall stay!"
But the Devil growing bored and having
        talent, in his way,
Mated demons with orang-outangs, and
        — here we are today.

[MUSTIQUE]

"Roll Up! Roll Up!"

Life is a terminal bungle,
Whatever you do — no-win;
We live in a zoo — in a jungle
Where the tigers are breaking *in.*

Life's an impossible circus,
The cavalry never arrive;
By accident — or on purpose,
No-one escapes alive!

[MUSTIQUE]

I am indebted to Peter de Vries for the fourth line.

A Glass Half Empty

Stands the glass half empty,
Or stands the glass half full?
Hand me the decanter, man,
I'll take another pull.

Stevie says that waving sets
The suckers up to drown.
Well, maybe so, but never let
The Bastards grind you down.

Stands the glass half empty,
Or stands the glass half full?
Cease you bloody banter, man,
I'll take another pull.

Oscar says a sinner gets
To wear a thorny crown.
I wouldn't know, but never let
The Bastards grind you down.

Stands the glass half empty,
Or stands the glass half full?
Blast your Buddhist mantra, man,
I'll take another pull.

Oxford says who holds the nets
In silence, wins renown.
He would say so! But never let
The Bastards grind you down.

Stands the glass half empty,
Or stands the glass half full?
Hand me the decanter, man,
I'll take another pull!

[MUSTIQUE]

For those who read little poetry — 'Stevie' is Stevie Smith; 'Oscar' is Oscar Wilde, and 'Oxford' is Edward de Vere, 17th Earl of Oxford.

Waste

Nobody weeps for the dead;
We might as well weep at a wall.
We weep for ourselves instead;
We weep for the waste of it all.

When flesh has frittered its term
We lower the bone in the ground;
Why do we serve to the worm
What is kept from the faithful hound?

Nobody mourns for the dead;
We mourn what we cannot recall.
We mourn for the word unsaid;
We mourn for the waste of it all.

[MUSTIQUE]

My intention to have my remains mummified and interred in a purpose-built pyramid has been the subject of much (richly deserved) merriment among friends and in various newspapers. It is only an idle, slightly ridiculous whim. Were my remains to be chopped up and fed to my wonderful rare-breed Gloucester Old Spot or Middle White pigs, I can't say it would bother me much. The lines above were inspired by a news item concerning a man and his dog trapped in a cave by snow. The dog had consumed his master's corpse. My reaction to this was very far from the vehement horror evinced in the article.

'You may not evil do...'

You may not evil do, that good be hurled
    To heal a greater wound. Upon such hope
Has balanced half the malice of the world,
    And toppled, headlong, down its fatal slope.

[MUSTIQUE]

In 1956, the philosopher, Elizabeth Anscombe (1919 -2001) objected to the conferment of an honorary degree upon ex-President Harry Truman (because of his decision to drop the atomic bomb on Hiroshima) with the words: 'You may not do evil that good may come.' The original expression, as far as I can trace it, came from *Some Fruits of Solitude* by William Penn (1644-1718), Quaker founder of Pennsylvania: 'To do evil that good may come of it is for bunglers in politics as well as morals.'

Here Be Dragons

We've mapped the mountains of the moon,
    The lava fields of mars,
We map the trails of migrant whales,
    We map the farthest stars.

We map the ocean's shifting shore,
    We've mapped the open sky,
The treasure rooms of Inca tombs
    And where the ley lines lie.

We map the spots upon the sun,
    We map the human gene;
The medics' knives took endless lives
    To map the soft machine.

We'd map the seven plains of hell
    If Satan gave the sign,
(All tyrants feed upon the need
    To move a dotted line).

We've mapped the bloody universe
    And pinned it in a net,
But as for charts of human hearts —
    We've made no progress yet!

[DORSINGTON]

Telling Lies

All the angels up in heaven
    Hang their shining heads to cry;
Even Santa Claus grows solemn
    When you tell your mum a lie.

And the fairies in the garden
    Who leave silver for your tooth,
They will whisper, if you ask them:
    'Always tell your mum the truth'.

If you don't believe in fairies,
    Or that reindeer ever flew,
You might murmur three Hail Marys
    For the lies your mum told you.

[DORSINGTON]

Dreams

For men to walk is but to fall, controlled;
For men to sleep is but rehearsing death.
Yet dreams are clay that slither from the mould,
No more can they be held than can a breath.

[SOHO]

Passing a School Playground

The imps are with the angels
   Behind the netted wall;
The squeals of pigtailed lassies,
   The thump of boot on ball.

A bookworm in a corner,
   The bully on his round,
Miss Showoff in her trainers
   That cost a hundred pound.

A murderer's among them,
   A few who'll make it rich,
Here's fame and shame in training,
   But God knows which is which.

[MUSTIQUE]

Last Words of Punch to Judy

'Philosophy is anybody's doxy —
(I always loved you, Judy, *entre nous*);
And yet we danced the jig of life by proxy:
The puppeteer was nobody we knew.'

[DORSINGTON]

'As I spied swallows scything...'

As I spied swallows scything
  Across an evening sky,
I thought upon those midges
  Whose turn it was to die.

Do midges boast of heroes?
  Are some born lame or halt?
Are geniuses among them
  To reckon blame or fault?

And as they swarm by millions
  In garden, field or fen,
Do midges mourn their fellows?
  Or do they die like men?

[DORSINGTON]

Five and a Bit

When
fully erect
the average dick
stands at five and a
bit inches tall. I have
no   information
to call on how
thick   such   a
hypothetical dick
might   sprawl;
still, taking a rule
of thumb and all,
and adding a tad,
robbing   Peter
for   Paul,
allowing for over
achievers   in
Gaul   and   the
pythons that lurk
in the halls of
Nepal, ignoring
what's scrawled
upon   lavatory
walls   and
omitting   those
eunuchs whose
data appals, I
submit ..... having
taken the matter
in hand ...... upon
measuring half
an inch up from
the balls, this is it!

[DORSINGTON]

The median size of an erect human penis is 5.08 inches according to that most excellent peri-
odical *New Scientist* in a recent article. Speaking personally, (and perhaps for a great many other
men), I am more than happy to belive them.

Sonnet for H20

[For Loren Eiseley]

Strange how the spark of life stirs not in fire,
Nor air, nor earth, but swims in viscous ooze
And shallow brine, its alchemy a weeping fuse
Of slime, a reeking womb propelled entire
By water. Water from a toxic mire,
From snowflakes, foaming brooks and morning dews,
From estuaries feeding silent deeps,
From marsh and mist and noon-dark monsoon rains.
Into the planet's molten heart, through veins
Of scoured rock and ice, earth's water creeps
And drips, and trickles, leaches, drains and seeps
Until, at last, past cave-blind fish, it gains
Once more the living Maine. And from some pool
Of warm, primaeval silt — produced this fool.

[DORSINGTON]

Loren Eiseley, for me the only scientist who ever wrote in a poet's tongue, deserves a far better sonnet than this. Sadly, it is the best that I can offer as my personal and sincere tribute to his memory. 'The Flow of the River' from his wonderful book *The Immense Journey* contains all the seeds of the above in prose that beggars description and shames my emulation. W.H. Auden in the *New Yorker* wrote of Eiseley: "I have eagerly read anything of his I could lay my hands on." So have I. And so should you, perhaps. Apart from *The Immense Journey*, I would also heartily recommend *The Star Thrower*, *The Unexpected Universe* and his stab at an autobiography, *All The Strange Hours*. Magical stuff!

Sonnet for Bob Dylan
On His 60th Birthday

In Juarez, where it never rains,
A weatherman with leather veins
Has bulldozed Desolation Row,
And franchised 'Tambourines-to-go'.
The Zimmerman's a Zimmer frame,
A tombstone in the Hall of Fame;
No shelter from the locust mob
Still howlin' *'Is it rollin', Bob?*
Still stealin' coal from Woody's dream?'
A loco' losin' heat and steam,
A slow train blowin' low and clear,
But I still play yr songs... y'hear?
   Them tracks were built on blood and gold —
   Damn, Bobby, how'd we get so old?

[DORSINGTON]

*[Thanks to two old friends: Don Atyeo who made me go back on my birthday
and write it all over again, and to Mick Farren — who didn't!]*

As a late 20th century songwriter Bob Dylan has no peer or rival. He stands alone, impossibly dominant, like a gaunt oak in a ravaged forest. Like many of my generation, I simply cannot imagine my life without his mumbled, whining, cynical wisdom as a consolatory soundtrack. Happy Birthday, Bob — ain't dark yet, but down the street the dogs are barking!

The Name of a Man

The name of a man is a numbing blow
   From which he never recovers,
(As mothers and monarchs and abbots know,
   Or passionate Valentine lovers).

The name of a thing is a pulley weight,
   A leash to throttle its thunder,
(As all of us finally learn too late,
   Revisiting infant wonder).

The name of a child is a second skin,
   You itch, but never outgrow it;
(To shed it, try naming yourself within,
   And never let anyone know it!)

[DORSINGTON]

The first two lines I owe to sixties media guru, Marshall McLuhan. As to abbots, monarchs, mothers and lovers — these are among the few people I could think of who may bestow new names on their fellow men, albeit that the latter are only divulged in newspaper Valentine announcements.

Executive Decisions

The car stood in the driveway,
　　The chauffeur at the gate;
I burst into her bedroom,
　　My watch said I was late.

I thought to find her sleeping,
　　To 'kiss-and-run' goodbye,
Instead, I found her towelling
　　Her tangled hair awry.

She smelt of sleep and flowers,
　　Her streaming flesh aglow.
My meetings were important;
　　Her towel moved to and fro...

The car and chauffeur waited,
　　While up in London town
Executive decisions
　　Were made as we lay down.

[SOHO]

I Never Met A Book...

[For Miles]

I no sooner see a book: I need it!
  (Even though I'll never read it),
    Books in any binding, any font;
Though it's always my ambition
  To acquire a *first* edition —
    I never met a book I didn't want!

Of my rivals in the chase: (God bless 'em!)
  How I long to dispossess 'em —
    Dreams of bookish burgling haunt my sleep,
Though the smell of vellum lingers
  On a dreaming felon's fingers —
    I never dreamt a book I didn't keep!

'Would you care to borrow this?': I have it!
  (Swear me out an affidavit!)
    Flattery finds fools who never learn;
Those who loan 'em — losers weepers!
  I disown 'em! Finders keepers! —
    I never took a book I could return!

[DORSINGTON]

One of my favourite anecdotes (Lord Chesterfield? Logan Pearsall Smith?) is of a father showing his son a particular part of his library while admonishing him: "Never lend books, my son. Only fools lend books. Once, all these books belonged to fools!"

In A Soho Garden

Here, in a Soho garden,
Secure from prying eyes,
I lounge in sultan splendour
And watch a spider rise
On threads of silken terror,
Scuttling with its prize
Beneath a fat geranium leaf
To parlours full of flies.

Here, in a Soho garden,
Where blackbirds sing like larks,
Four stories from the alleys
Where foxes shoal like sharks,
I water my geraniums
In floodlit, silver arcs:
Downstairs, the foxes dance on chairs,
While bouncers strip the marks.

[DORSINGTON]

I have lived in the same Soho flat in London for thirty years now on the top floor of a court built
in the late eighteenth century. My 'rooftop garden', by the way, is about the size of a kingsize bed,
but I do have a resident blackbird! And could somebody tell me where all the bees come from
in spring and summer? 'Foxes' is old cockney slang (rhymes with doxies) for ladies of the night
who entice 'marks' (customers) into dodgy nightclubs. I never have seen a real fox *(Vulpes vulpes)*
in Soho itself, but other residents claim they have.

Ts'ai Lun at Ch'in Che'eng

At Ch'in Che'eng, by the river bank,
In squalor sits Ts'ai Lun — alone:
Bereft of honour, stripped of rank,
With only enemies to thank,
He gnaws an exile's bone.

His lacquered nails but filthy jags,
A scented bath his only wish,
His splendid robes mere threadbare rags,
He rests upon his saddle bags
And watches peasants fish.

'Outfoxed, Ts'ai Lun! You fat-arsed fool!'
Unspoken thoughts. His servant nods
And rises from his broken stool
To serve a bowl of rice and gruel:
'A feast fit for the gods!'

'So tell me, Chan, across the bay,
What is it these poor wretches smelt
In giant cauldrons night and day?'
Chan sucks his teeth: 'My Lord, they say
That what they make is felt.'

The weeks drag by as Ts'ai Lun learns
Of matted fibres, wool and hair,
And peers within great leaden urns
Or stands beside the groaning churns,
His head bowed, as in prayer.

At last, the outcast courtier calls
For bark and cloth of any kind,
Old fishing nets, his cast-off shawls,
A bale of hemp, Chan's overalls...
Ts'ai Lun has lost his mind!

For many a weary hour, in wrath
Men heat and pound the eunuch's mix,
To strain away the stinking froth
And rend the useless boiling broth
With hunting knives and sticks.

Meanwhile, Ts'ai Lun elects a crew
To work a far yet stranger task,
To build a mesh of split bamboo
Upon a frame. Chan wonders 'Who
Will be the first to ask?'

A village elder rolls his eye
As Ts'ai Lun draws a weary breath,
'Come, old one, do you wonder why
We labour?' 'Nay,' comes the reply,
'My Lord, I seek not death!

'But skilled am I this many a-year
In felt, both in its shape and form.
With due respect, My Lord, I fear
No matter how we struggle here
Such cloth will keep none warm.'

Ts'ai's laughter rolls across the bay,
One hand upon his heaving breast,
He wipes the streaming tears away
And taps his startled protegé:
'I thank you for the jest!

The work will warm us, more or less!'
He waddles to the vats again,
The mesh is raised, a sodden mess
Transported to an ancient press
And washed by puzzled men.

Wrung out to dry at Ts'ai's command
A flimsy sheet is smoothed and curled,
Propelled by Chan's unsteady hand
Against a wall and gently fanned:
The 'felt' that changed the world!

At Ch'in Che'eng, where the river bends,
Each year they hold a grand parade,
The Lord Ts'ai Lun *(old Chan attends!)*
Sends greetings to his serfs and friends
Where paper first was made.

[soho]

That Chief Eunuch Ts'ai Lun was the inventor of paper during the Han dynasty is well documented, despite his virtual absence from Western encyclopaedias. Exiled for some long forgotten intrigue at court to a remote province where they manufactured felt, Ts'ai Lun produced the first known sheet of paper, dried on a peasant's wall, in 105 AD or thereabouts. It was made mostly of bark and hemp. He was later raised to the nobility. The use of paper instead of silk (expensive) or bamboo (bulky) in the trade, educational, administrative and military fields cemented China's absolute dominance of Asia for the next thousand years. Ts'ai Lun is as close at it gets to being the most influential man who ever lived.

'The jacket Elvis loaned me...'

The jacket Elvis loaned me
  When I was nearly ten,
Still hangs inside my closet.
  I brush it now and then.

The specs I got from Buddy
  When I was just a kid
Don't suit me like they used to.
  Perhaps they never did.

The boots of Spanish leather
  From Bobby D's first love
Have lasted half a lifetime.
  They fit me like a glove!

[DORSINGTON]

Victory!

We fought for Peace and carried her, protesting
  To battle, where we slaughtered, with much blood,
Her enemies. Their chieftains died contesting
  Her remnant pieces, quartered in the mud.

[NEW YORK]

America

This tribe, I know —
        from having dwelt so long within its tents
And found it so,
        that jests or common sense discharge no rents;
That fools in bells
        might snatch a bone, but still must sleep on straw,
That minstrel hells
    were welcome in their place — but little more.

Yet who am I —
        to shoo such wooly sheep from shiny shelves?
Nor should I cry
        for fools to salvage culture from themselves;
The choice is theirs,
        and nothing less than fear can force that trick —
(In neighbour's lairs,
        Our speech is soft who carry no big stick).

The sad pretense,
        that they know best, when what they know is dross;
Their innocence
        that dooms the sullen world to blood and loss;
Their startled plea
        that lesser tribes will neither pray nor vote:
They will not see
        nor look — until the wolves are at their throat.

Their scale-eyed chief,
    a priest who balms the rich and pays no tax;
Their odd belief
    that half the world makes mime behind their backs;
Who truly know,
    that what the world needs most is shopping malls;
Both friend and foe,
    beyond their ken — 'til death or duty calls;

Yet contrawise,
    what people gifted strangers half so much?
And damn their eyes,
    when friends are lepers, ingrates shun to touch;
So here we stand,
    and though our own tribe's ju-ju men play dumb,
At your command,
    hearts full of doubt — America — we come!

[NEW YORK CITY]

America has done more for me financially than Britain ever has, or ever could have done. Even when on its worst behaviour, I find myself automatically defending the USA from the sneers of green-eyed Europhiles playing their Greek trumps to Roman aces. America is an empire. All empires, by definition, are bumbling, shambolic, bullying, bureaucratic affairs — as certain of the rightness of their cause in infancy as they are corrupted by power in their dotage. I am no historian, but it seems to me that the sins of the USA, compared to those of most previous empires, are of a more moderate — if more pervasive — kind. To put it bluntly, if Americans are so fat, stupid and ignorant, how come they rule the world?

The Meeting

The hierarchy meets once or twice a year here,
Their bundles and their papers underarm.
    Some come hearty, some come sure,
    Some come striding through the door,
Genuflecting, radiating charm.
    Some come mincing in like whores,
    Some come wary, (some have cause),
And some send their regrets to keep from harm.

The price of compromise is somewhat dear here;
Here is where ambition slips its sheath.
    Some are cunning, some are wise,
    Some are here to patronise,
Some sit grinning, lying through their teeth.
    Some are crawling sycophants,
    Some mere courtiers at the dance,
Some carrying bouquets — and some a wreath.

"Is there any other business we must clear here?"
A rush of voices babble juxtaposed.
    Some still yet to make their marks,
    Some still circling like sharks,
Claiming points of order unopposed.
    Some still seeking an alliance,
    Some still whining in defiance...
"In that case, I declare this meeting closed."

[DORSINGTON]

Misery Guts

Each to his own, Monsieur. Our debt
   Remains to those whom hope bereaves.
The weeds of dreams spring stronger yet
   As tyrants stamp among the leaves.

The more they scythe, the more they thresh,
   The further thistledown is cast,
And, *à la fin*, it shoots afresh,
   To seed the whole wide world, at last.

My father and his messmates, too,
   Spat out defeat, and undeterred
Fought on for misery guts, like you —
   Who never spoke a German word!

[SOHO]

Egocentric, autocratic, arrogant; all words inextricably connected with the French novelist and dramatist Henry de Montherlant (1896 - 1972). His scathing attacks on feminist sentiment and influence in modern life were beneath contempt — as was his reaction to German victory in 1940, which he considered 'a salutary lesson' to French democracy. But there is no doubting the power of Montherlant's prose. In short, a brilliant, nasty piece of work who confirms the theory that there is no correlation whatever between talent and congeniality. He took his own life, fearing blindness, aged 76 in Paris. I must here admit that I was unable to discover whether Henry de Montherlant spoke German or not. At least he never had to do so by government decree as he might well have been forced to do if my father's generation had listened to his defeatist, clever-dick blather.

Queen Elizabeth I Greets A Lord

The exiled courtier creeps into the crowd,
An age has passed since last he ventured here;
'So long my lord?' his monarch hails aloud,
'We had forgot the fart this many a year!'

[NEW YORK]

An oft repeated if apocryphal story... Having committed an unpardonable breach of etiquette in the royal personage's presence, Edward de Vere, Earl of Oxford, exiled himself for seven years from the court of Queen Elizabeth — only to face this greeting on his return. I am indebted to Lord Litchfield for this amusing anecdote from Aubrey's *Brief Lives*.

Though fondness may not fall within our gift...'

Though fondness may not fall within our gift,
And greater love be colour
to the blind,
Yet still a man may anchor evil's drift,
If writ upon his tomb is:
He Was Kind

[DORSINGTON]

Udde~Well Pond

Old Udde-Well Pond is dark and deep,
Its waters shunned by tup and sheep;
The haunt of badger, fox and deer,
Of silent pools and nameless fear.

The black bricked well is running still
Though none come now to drink their fill;
Udde's odd name carved upon the spout.
White crosses keep the witches out.

A thousand years on muddy tracks,
With yokes and buckets on their backs,
Folk fetched the water up Welsh Hill,
And left the kine to drink their fill.

Now, pond and well lie wild, forlorn,
Forgotten, bound in rush and thorn;
I've heard that once, in cruel despair,
A young lass drowned her sorrows there.

[DORSINGTON]

In the Blood?

Nature or nurture or... Nietzsche?
Are we writ in the stars, or in clay?
Are the features of each of Gods creatures
Held ransom in random decay?

As Darwin sat scribbling his thesis
Of barnacles, beagles and men,
Was it predestination of species
Which guided the strokes of his pen?

Implacable as the creator,
The demons that urge us to mate;
Mother Nature's an iron dictator —
To multiply is to mutate.

It's wicked to think of, it's vicious,
But some kids are born little shits;
Before they can crawl they're malicious;
Rotten eggs sucking on tits.

Abandon the thought if you want, sir.
I leave it to parents to choose;
But I know of *one* little monster —
Please never ask me whose!

[DORSINGTON]

Specific Gravity

Though kith and kin may sacrifice their life,
    Though loyalty be bred into the bone,
Though God may bind together man and wife —
    Yet still the minds of men must quest alone.

Bequeath your children all the books you please,
    Or lead a horse to water in a drought —
The doors of revelation have their keys,
    Yet none may force the portal from without.

'Aye, nowt as strange as folk,' the Yorkies say,
    And said it since Neanderthal napped stone;
Though men join hands to ease each other's way —
    Yet still the mind of man quests on... alone.

[DORSINGTON]

Intentions

What's an intention? A scarecrow of straw
Stuffed full of guilt in a field of
sighs.
My! How the crows of reality caw,
Perched on its head, as they peck out its
eyes.

[MUSTIQUE]

[85]

How To Get Rich

Good fortune? The fact is
The more that you practise,
The harder you sweat,
The luckier you get.

Ideas? We've had 'em
Since Eve mated Adam,
But take it from me
Execution's the key.

The money? Just pester
A likely investor.
To get what you need
You toady to greed.

The talent? Go sign it!
But first, wine and dine it.
It's tedious work
With a talented jerk.

Good timing? To win it
You gotta be in it.
Just never be late
To quit or cut bait.

Expansion? It's vanity!
Profit is sanity.
Overhead begs
To walk on two legs.

The first step? Just do it
And bluff your way thru' it.
Remember to duck!
God speed...
and good luck!

[MUSTIQUE]

Space Craft

'Nous appelons notre avenir l'ombre de lui-même que notre passé projette devant nous.'
'What we call our future is the shadow which the past throws in front of us.'
— *Marcel Proust*

Like new loosed heifers, sleek and lean,
All winter held in barns close pinned,
We yearn for grass which none have seen,
Our small craft straws upon the wind —
Where no wind blows. And some, they say,
Have tombs which tumbled not to earth
But in the glare of endless day
Spin rudderless, the Void their berth,
Their solar wings and crippled sails
Computing readouts none can use,
While flocks of man-made nightingales
Sing out alerts to long-dead crews.

Yet whether from a weightless womb
Or from the vats of alchemy,
These words shall sound a planet's doom:
'A *child is born in Zero-G*'.

[CANDLEWOOD]

[87]

'Hail to the gods of America...'

Hail to the gods of America!
Hail to the gods of the Dream,
Invictus! *'E Pluribus Unum'*!
But which of them reigns supreme?

Which is America's Jupiter?
The brahmins of Capitol Hill?
A sorcerous prophet on Wall Street?
The eye of a Dollar bill?

Or is it it Celebrity Status —
The worship of those we hate,
Or the cult of Living Forever
If only we'd watch our weight?

What of the titans of Media,
Or Hollywood's siren call;
What of the temples of Justice
Whose servants enslave us all?

What of the Brand and the Label?
What of the upstart Sport?
And what of the Constitution,
That bully of last resort?

Hail to the God of America
Whose power the masses extol —
Convenience rules America;
Convenience owns our soul.

[SOHO]

'All the young dudes...'

All the young dudes, growin' old,
   Wanna get their story told,
Wanna see their names in print,
   Write a bio'— make a mint.

All the young dudes, wearin' specs,
   Waitin' on retirement cheques,
Takin' stairlifts up to heaven —
   Lift broke back in 'sixty-seven.

All the young dudes, gettin' frail,
   Hair a whiter shade of pale,
Thinkin' back to glory days,
   Memories a purple haze.

All the young dudes, short on cash,
   Hittin' wine insteada hash,
Got no use for LSD —
   Drugs come from the pharmacy.

All the young dudes — cut to fade,
   Gettin' limp insteada laid,
Life's a bitch and two's a crowd —
   Crank the volume way up loud.

[MUSTIQUE]

To those of us of a certain age, 1967 was...everything. Call it the summer of love. Call it the high point of sex 'n' drugs 'n' rock 'n' roll. Call it any damn thing you want, but if you weren't there, especially in London or San Francisco...you wouldn't understand. Me? I was wandering up and down the Kings Road, Chelsea, with a snake-hipped, suede-booted blonde in white lipstick and spider web eyelashes, dressed myself in a full length military cloak and chiffon scarf, hair half way down my arse, imbibing green tea and hash in a hangout near World's End. Hey, for a 20 year old South London dude, it didn't get any cooler than that!

Eureka!

To know a thing that no man knew before,
To know, and know no other soul suspects;
Happier those, perhaps, marooned ashore —
The sea of truth is littered with such wrecks.

[MUSTIQUE]

An IBM Engineer
Makes A Service Call

"Twelve for the gypsies, eight for the Jews,
  And three for the nancies — please excuse
    my French!

"Nein! Not a nursery rhyme, *(you arse!)*
  It's a mnemonic — could you pass
    my wrench?

"There, by the cover plate, jammed in hard,
  Wrapped on the spin-shaft drive...it's a card,
    well creased.

"Right. Let's decipher the punch-card hole:
  This would suggest the code...for a Pole,
    deceased.

"Date of confinement here at the camp
    Is out of alignment; cross-sort stamp
        is clear.

"Code five, (suicide), assigned code six;
    Automatic reject — made two nicks,
        just here.

"Input defective across this line:
    ± Prisoner ± female ± Jew ± aged nine ±
        — wrong file.

"A clerical balls-up; what's new there!
    She's done. Just sign by the cross, mein Herr.
        Sieg Heil!"

[DORSINGTON]

'To meet Hitler's requirements, IBM devised a racial census which listed not only religious affilia-tions, but also bloodlines. ....Every prisoner — known only by a number — was identified with a card, with holes and columns detailing nationalities, date of birth, work skills, and reason for incar-ceration. Hole three signified homosexual; hole 12 was for gypsy; hole eight for Jew. Column 34 was labelled 'Reason for Departure'. Code two meant transferred. Suicide was coded five. And code six was designated 'special handling' — the term used for extermination, whether in a gas chamber or by gunshot.... For IBM, such work was highly profitable....The first IBM factory was built in Germany and more than 2000 machines were distributed across the country. IBM staff trained the Nazis to use them; they set up offices, and produced the 1.5 billion punch cards used every year in Germany alone. They also serviced the machines on a monthly basis — sometimes travelling to concentration camps to do so.....After the war, while the perpetrators of the Holocaust were being rounded up for trial, IBM New York recovered its machines, leased them instead to the allies, and quietly assimilated its wartime profits.' — Extract from *The Week* (UK) 24th February 2001 quoting the new book *IBM and the Holocaust* by Edwin Black, published by Little, Brown.

Sylva Anathema

[So curses every tree felled by man]

From the first flint stroke
    These apes called folk
        Have ravaged their hearts' desire;

Our forests awoke
    To flame and smoke
        At the hour they captured fire.

As the seasons turn
    They axe and burn,
        And Weald gives way to plough;

So few of us stand,
    The wounded land
        Lies stripped of root and bough.

I am marked to fall
    But warn them all
        That what they reap, they'll rue;

When their bones are dust...
    Their axes rust...
        We shall cover the earth anew.

[DORSINGTON]

Hunting Monsters

[A shanty for the US Department of Homeland Security]

We fish them up from murky seas
  As orcas hunt a porpoise,
We shape our hooks from liberties,
  The oars from habeus corpus.

Like Ahab on some phantom quest,
  We flee where few pursue us,
We lecture friends who loved us best,
  And spit on those who knew us.

In grief and rage we flense our cause,
  No mercy and no quarter;
Harpooning laws on foreign shores,
  Their oil the spoil of slaughter.

Some songs are older than the Ark,
  And, if you wish, I'll hum one:
When hunting monsters in the dark,
  Take care, lest you become one.

[MUSTIQUE]

'He who fights with monsters might take care lest he thereby become a monster.' — Friedrich
Nietzsche, Jenseits von Gut und Böse (1886)

Shields

Warrior, know your shield a two-edged weight,
Constricting as it blocks the killing blow.
The drawn bridge bars escape by Western gate,

While ramparts hide besiegers far below;
Thus sanctuary is turned to blazing trap,
And iron armour freezes in the snow.

All shields exact the price of handicap,
No turtle ever raced the wind-borne hare,
Nor porcupine e'er nestled in a lap.

No woman ever held me in her snare
To pierce my heart with tenderness as bait,
To bring me squalling brats to call my heir.

I stand before you now, inviolate.
Warrior! Know your shield a two-edged weight!

[DORSINGTON]

Amazing Grace

[for Rear Admiral Grace Murray Hopper]

A counter-clockwise clock:
   Tock-tick, tock-tick, tick-tock.
     The budget's chock-a-block,
      The project's in dry dock.

Abandon ship? Who'll tell her
   She's fouled her own propeller?
     You'll need ear-plugs young fellah —
      She's a salty Cinderella!

Amazing Grace won't buy it,
   (It's not that she'll *defy* it):
     "If questioned, just deny it,
      But, whatever happens — *try it!*"

[MUSTIQUE]

Strange that one of the most inspirational people I have ever read about should be a Rear Admiral in the US Navy. Grace Murray Hopper was the co-inventor of COBOL, an important early computer programming language which made it possible to instruct computers using words rather than numbers. Her survival and rise in the male dominated world of the US armed forces speaks volumes for her abilities and guts. Hopper was a legend in the American Navy when she retired 'involuntarily' aged eighty, after 43 years of service. She was often credited with launching or supporting what appeared to her superiors to be 'hare-brained schemes' — only to be vindicated later. These ideas included using computers to track the life cycle of crop eating locusts, building a weather computer and tracking the waves at the bottom of the ocean. She smoked unfiltered Lucky Strike cigarettes and kept a clock in her office that ran counter-clockwise, to remind herself time was 'running out' rather than 'going by'. There are many versions of the famous sign on her desk. I chose years ago to make one of them the official motto of my publishing company: "If it's a good idea, go ahead and do it. It's much easier to apologise than it is to get permission." She died in 1992 aged 85.

[97]

'Shadow Billy'

"By God, I wish that I
Were twenty-five year younger.
I'd blacken up yer eye!
There's not a man among yer!"

The bouncers put him right
And sent him down the 'Dilly:
"He does it every night —
They call him 'Shadow Billy'.

"He wouldn't hurt a fly,"
They grinned in recollection —
"That is, unless his eye
Detects his own reflection!"

[MUSTIQUE]

'Shadow Billy' was a Soho character in the middle 80's, well known to bouncers, coppers and door-men alike. He only ever attacked his own reflection. The 'Dilly is Piccadilly Circus, of course.

Trouble

Out of the mail, your mouth still yawning,
    Out of the phone by your bed at night,
Out of the blue on a glorious morning,
    Suddenly, everything's *not* alright.
        Trouble. Trouble.
    Suddenly, everything's not alright.

Out of the mouth of a friendly stranger,
    Out of the crease of a lover's frown,
Out of the cry of a child in danger,
    Suddenly, everything's upside-down.
        Trouble. Trouble.
    Suddenly, everything's upside-down.

Out of a rain of boots and curses,
    Out of the barrel of some fool's gun,
Out of the eyes of hospital nurses,
    Suddenly, everything's come undone.
        Trouble. Trouble.
    Everything under the sun — undone.

[MUSTIQUE]

An Old Dog Is The Best Dog

An old dog is the best dog,
A dog with rheumy eyes;
An old dog is the best dog
A dog grown sad and wise,
    Not one who snaps at bubbles,
        Nor one who barks at nowt,
            A dog who knows your troubles,
              A dog to see you out.

An old bitch is the best bitch,
Not pups to fetch your sticks;
An old bitch is the best bitch,
Not one to teach new tricks,
    Not one who's up and leaping,
        But one whose coat is grey,
            Leg's twitching while she's sleeping
              In dreams of yesterday.

[MUSTIQUE]

The Proof

[For Dick Pountain]

Knowledge comes but hard and slow,
　　And much is hid that once we knew.
Much there is we cannot know;
　　Or, if we know, we misconstrue.

Gods are built on faith and prayer,
　　And faith demands divinity;
Math alone is truth laid bare,
　　The proof of all infinity.

Prime is prime, no ifs or buts,
　　Immutable as '3', '1', '7';
You do not 'feel it in your guts':
　　Prime on earth ***is*** prime in heaven.

[MUSTIQUE]

In his amusing biography of Paul Erdös *The Man Who Loved Only Numbers*, Paul Hoffman quotes the number theorist G. H. Hardy on the beauty and rigour of numbers which he believed 'constitute the true fabric of the universe.' Hardy postulated that the mathematician 'is in much more direct contact with reality [than a physicist] who deals with the subject matter usually described as 'real'. 317 is a prime, not because we think it is so, or because our minds are shaped in one way rather than another, but because it is so, because mathematical reality is built that way.'

Spot The Difference

One marvels at
   the infinite variety of souls
      who crew this ship of fools,
         adrift upon an endless sea —

Sans chart or map,
   the rotting superstructure shot with holes,
      while with their toy-town tools
         men launch the lifeboats endlessly.

Or is it that
   the superstructure rots within our souls
      while endless drifts of fools
         of infinite variety —

Their maps aflap,
   in shot-up ships, chart out on lifeboat shoals,
      sans crew, their toy-town rules
         to launch into eternity?

[MUSTIQUE]

'When mercy strains your patience...'
[For Steve and Lynn Caldwell]

When mercy strains your patience, son,
    When strangers ask for more,
When common sense says you have done
    Enough — throw wide your door!

'The world is too much with us' said
    The poet — he was wise:*
Why miss the chance of breaking bread
    With angels in disguise?

[MUSTIQUE]

*'The world is too much with us; late and soon,
 Getting and spending, we lay waste our powers:'
— William Wordsworth

'Knowing isn't doing...'

Knowing isn't doing if there's nothing to be done;
Doing minus knowing's only bluffing on the run;
    Knowing isn't doing;
    Doing isn't knowing;
Nothing but the knowing plus the doing gets it done.

[HIGHFIELD]

The Wedding Dress

The woodland trees are decked in reds,
The scarlet blush of newly-weds
Impatient on their wedding night —
Fresh-minted gold their shy delight.

Now jilted summer stands aside
As autumn claims his burning bride,
Arrayed in all her finery,
Displayed for all the world to see.

But honeymoons are short, if sweet,
And time flies by on raptured feet;
Too soon a tyrant's icy stare
Will fall upon fair limbs laid bare.

So I will walk in autumn mist
To see the bride before she's kissed,
Collecting up her leaves to press
A memory — her wedding dress.

[DORSINGTON]

The Troubles

As I was passing Dublin Gate,
I met a man who dined on hate,
  Who supped upon a sea of song
Made bitter by an ancient wrong.

As I passed through a Belfast mist,
I met a man who shook his fist,
  Who preyed upon the men of hate
Who crept at night through Dublin Gate.

As I was passing Cromwell Street,
I met a man blown off his feet,
  Who scrawled in blood upon a stone:
No prisoners! God will know His own!

As I was passing Parliament,
I met a man whose orders sent
  Young squaddies out upon the street
To shoot at men they'd never meet.

As I was passing New York State,
I met a man who heaped a plate
  With others' pain; who paid a fee
To be a part of history.

As I passed by a widow's door
I heard a cry: *Dear Christ, no more!*
  A pox upon your Dublin Gate,
Your Belfast mist... your men of hate.

[NEW YORK]

Dead White Males

They tell me that postmodernism's in the saddle now,
Having swapped its thoroughbred to mount a sacred cow;
Laying waste the landscape of a culture as it rails
In righteous deconstruction of...
    Dead White Males.

They tell me indiscriminate discrimination rules;
Eurocentric rubbish has been scoured from our schools;
There's no room in curriculums for sexist fairy tales
To sow the seeds of tyrannies from...
    Dead White Males.

They tell me multicultural academies must rid
Their blushing shelves of Shakespeare — or Chaucer, God forbid!
For Raleigh, Swift and Dickens and Wordsworth in his dales,
Walt Whitman, Donne and Tennyson are...
    Dead White Males.

Envoi
    "D.W.M.s,
Chuck 'em in the Thames.
Plait a rope and string a gallows,
To the libraries! Wheelbarrows!
Strip the stacks of books by liars —
Shred 'em! Hurl 'em in the fires!
That'll learn 'em, those who wrote 'em,
Saw their balls off at the scrotum!
Fetch a hammer! Fetch the nails!
Crucify all
 Dead White Males!"

"A minefield of unimaginable minorities waiting to be offended" — Harold Evans on American Universities. Political Correctness of any stripe starts with the best of intentions — as a clarion call. It then passes through various stages — as an irritating background whine or strident name-calling, for instance — until, at last, it emerges as the massed braying of lunatic donkeys. Unfortunately, all that is needed for the adherents of this New Ignorance to wield real power is for people to do nothing. In an age of information technology, sticks and stones <u>can</u> break your bones!

The Serpent's Gift

I dissemble,
You dissemble,
We dissemble,
Lying straight, or slantly by omission;
   So, will the Prince of Liars
   Cast us all into the fires
As punishment? Or are we competition?

See no evil?
Speak no evil?
Hear no evil?
'Lord, not yet!' Augustine's hollow vow.
   The Magi in their trammels
   Dreamt of sherbet, not of camels;
Holy hermits know the 'why' but not the 'how'.

'Little liar!'
'Pants on fire!'
'Porky-pie-er!'
When creeps deceit into a child's mind;
   And are their fibs acquired,
   Or do they come hard-wired?
Are the mouths of babes the sum of humankind?

I dissemble,
You dissemble,
We dissemble;
A veil of lies to cloak a vale of tears;
   A camouflage of kindness,
   The serpent's gift of blindness;
The cataracts that soften wasted years.

[CANDLEWOOD]

A Poet's Consolation

Beside broad streams of hieroglyphic flood
   The battlements of prose are raised in vain;
Their clay decays, subsiding into mud —
   While diamond shards of verse alone remain.

[SOHO]

Dream Time

Within a dream I watched a city rise
   To thrive a thousand years in craft and power,
And mourned to see its wreck through god-like eyes:
   Yet woke to find I'd slept but half an hour.

Time tramples on, the years roll by in ranks
   No less upon the wicked than the blessed,
How is it then that dreams, like armoured tanks,
   Reverse the trick, their centuries compressed?

[CANDLEWOOD]

'The House that Crack Built...'

This is the house that crack built.

This is the pipe
That lay in the house that crack built.

This is the puff,
That filled the pipe
That lay in the house that crack built.

This is the stuff,
That would not puff,
That filled the pipe
That lay in the house that crack built.

This is the sod,
That sold the stuff,
That would not puff,
That filled the pipe
That lay in the house that crack built.

This is the gun with the barrel sawn,
That shot the sod,
That sold the stuff,
That would not puff,
That filled the pipe
That lay in the house that crack built.

This is the room with the curtains drawn
That hid the gun with the barrel sawn,
That shot the sod,
That sold the stuff,
That would not puff,
That filled the pipe
That lay in the house that crack built.

This is the man who slept at dawn,
That lived in the room with the curtains drawn,
That sold the gun with the barrel sawn,
That shot the sod,
That sold the stuff,
That would not puff,
That filled the pipe
That lay in the house that crack built.

This is the frock all tattered and torn,
That kept the man who slept at dawn,
That lived in the room with the curtains drawn,
That sold the gun with the barrel sawn,
That shot the sod,
That sold the stuff,
That would not puff,
That filled the pipe
That lay in the house that crack built.

This is the maiden all forlorn,
That wore the frock all tattered and torn,
That kept the man who slept at dawn,
That lived in the room with the curtains drawn,
That sold the gun with the barrel sawn,
That shot the sod,
That sold the stuff,
That would not puff,
That filled the pipe
That lay in the house that crack built.

This is the babe that never was born,
That died in the womb of a maid forlorn,
That wore the frock all tattered and torn,
That kept the man who slept at dawn,
That lived in the room with the curtains drawn,
That sold the gun with the barrel sawn,
That shot the sod,
That sold the stuff,
That would not puff,
That filled the pipe
That lay in the house that crack built.

[MUSTIQUE]

I know only too well of what I speak in this poem. My advice to anyone about to try crack is as follows: Firstly, it will cost you more than you can pay. Secondly, it will play havoc with your health in a very short time. Thirdly, because your personality will change, most of your friends will disown you — just as you will lose interest in anyone not taking or selling crack. Fourthly, you will almost certainly become addicted (and super-paranoid) very quickly indeed. Lastly, unless you quit early (difficult) and permanently (very, very difficult) the lifestyle and the drug itself will conspire to kill you. Apart from all that, it's great!

Skate Mates

The gang's all here along the shore;
My toes a-tingle, fingers raw,
I buckle up my skates and make
A prayer to Thaw, the god of war.

I fly across the frozen lake
Without a handlebar or brake,
Carving curves with nerves of steel.
Look what an acrobat I'd make!

Colliding into Billy Teale,
Who tumbles like a Catherine wheel,
I wonder what the fish below
Would make of Billy as a meal!

Scooping up some snow to throw
A snowball at a girl I know,
We intertwine and fall down, slow.
Her hand in mine — it's time to go!

[CANDLEWOOD]

[113]

Gulliver Sneesby

Gulliver Sneesby, child of shame,
  Deplored that he was born a fella,
He tried and tried to change his name
  To Isabella.

Gulliver played the bore at large,
  A feminist in tyrant's clothing;
He wore his zeal to camouflage
  His own self-loathing.

Gulliver wrestled, wracked with guilt,
  Tormented by debased desires;
He fantasized himself rebuilt,
  With surgeon's pliers.

Gulliver scoured the dictionary
  While etymologists debated,
He wanted half the OED
  To be castrated.

Gulliver sneered at marriage vows,
  As 'sexist tricks to chain and fetter',
He sighed for those pathetic cows
  Who knew nno better.

Gulliver Sneesby, mother's son,
  A prophet who gained little credit;
He wrote a tome that weighed a ton,
  But no-one read it.

[CANDLEWOOD]

Apologies to Edward Arlington Robinson and his masterpiece, Miniver Cheevy. Whenever I am down, I only have to think of the lines: "He missed the medieval grace / Of iron clothing" to put me to rights. I must apologise, too, to Guy Sneesby, the internet genius at Dennis Interactive in London. Guy is absolutely nothing like the wretch described above, but I simply could not resist using his family name. (Note: OED: The Oxford English Dictionary. The 'definitive historical dictionary of the English language')

Why Do They Do It?

['I could never be a politician. I couldn't bear to
be right all the time.' — Sir Peter Ustinov]

Why do they do it? Why do they do it?
Why do they stand on their hind legs lying —
Lying and lying and lying and lying —
Even though everyone knows that they do it?
Even though everyone mutters: I knew it!
I knew it, I knew it! I <u>*knew*</u> they were lying!
Lying when even their mothers aren't buying.
How can they do it?   *How* can they do it?
Spinning a web til they're lost in the thick of it,
Topping the knob til we're all of us sick of it,
Sick of the pack of 'em, spouters and stammerers,
Whining in microphones, preening for cameras,
Bullying, blaming and always denying —
And lying and lying and lying and *lying*.

[DORSINGTON]

[115]

A Lullaby for Bottles

Here we lie in stony quiet,
Far below the lamplit halls,
Troubled not by human riot,
Safe within our weeping walls.

Here is comfort, here is nectar.
Here is comradeship compressed.
Here lie we, the vine's protector,
While the fruit of ages rest.

Sleep my brethren, dream and sleep,
Row on row and line by line;
You have promises to keep,
You who guard the living wine.

[SOHO]

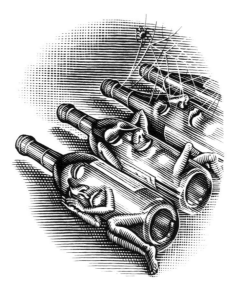

The Ballad of Madeleine

[Californian Gold Rush : 1851]

Along a rocky mountain track, grim faced and dusty-eyed,
A Frenchman and an Englishman were walking side by side,
Both arguing the toss concerning which of them should ride
Their last surviving donkey — at stake was national pride!

'Mon Dieu, m'sieur', the Frenchie said, 'we 'ave no time to lose!
Zis donkeyz name is Madeleine, as French as Fort Toulouse;
Am I to *walk* while rosbif rides and polishes 'is shoes?
Non, non, m'sieur, I much prefer we let ze *donkey* choose!'

The Englishman took off his hat to fan his face and smile,
He knew Jacques's reputation for cunning and for guile,
But still, he loved a bet, and coming up in double file,
'You're on!' he cried. 'Let's find a spot to put it to the trial!'

He waited for his wily friend to drop the reins, then said:
'So now we each take turns to call?' Jean-Jacques inclined his head;
The Frenchie's plan was well prepared, his pockets full of bread —
A juicy feast to tempt the beast. Instead, she turned and fled!

In vain they chased young Madeleine for mile on empty mile,
But never did catch up with her — and never will — meanwhile,
She reached a forty-niner's mine who'd found a golden pile:
While Englishmen and Frenchmen fight, the Yankees rides in style!

[MUSTIQUE]

'Oh, do not call them vultures...'

Oh, do not call them vultures, for vultures love dead meat
And rarely don disguises or lurk across the street.
Not so your tabloid journalist who craves his victims fresh,
To feed the willing multitudes who lust for living flesh.

Oh, do not call them jackals, such epithets are crude,
A journo slays for shillings, a jackal hunts for food.
No more are they hyenas; hyenas do not laugh
While nosing through their vomit for one last paragraph.

Oh, do not call them leeches, they've heard all that before,
And leeches have their uses — they gorge upon a war;
They worship trains derailing, they feast on plague or flood:
Yet were we to ignore them, they'd fade for lack of blood!

[DORSINGTON]

Scapegoats

Men smile at superstitions, fingers crossed —
    Barabbas rapped on wood — they let him go.
Yet Pontius Pilate diced with Christ and lost —
    All scapegoats have their uses — cross or no.

[MUSTIQUE]

Prodigal Son

Often I ventured in Babylon's towers,
        Never a friend I met — never a one,
        Playing the part of the prodigal son.
Many the weeks and many the hours,
Barely a moment to think of the flowers
        Patiently budding in Warwickshire's air.
        Never a thought of a snapdragon there,
Or May on the hedge. All of my powers
        Spent upon gilding the lilies of gain,
While blue-eyed forget-me-nots lowered their gaze,
        Their beauty unmourned in an English lane.
Yet now, as I lie amidst Babylon's maze,
        Decked in the trappings of fabulous dross,
        By the sirens of night, I weep for their loss.

[NEW YORK]

'I had a friend...'

I had a friend whom once I thought I knew,
Yet no man knows another's heart, entire;
He killed himself and damn near killed me, too —
The dead are no less dead by friendly fire.

[MUSTIQUE]

[119]

The Fool

My friend would ask me, curious,
   When we were lads in school,
'You know it makes 'em furious,
   Why play the bloody fool?'

My mother she would scold me
   Or lecture me in tears;
How many times she told me
   To emulate my peers.

When I was one and twenty,
   My editor would say:
'You've talent here aplenty,
   Why play the fool all day?'

And even my true lover
   In gentleness will ask,
'I love you like no other,
   Think you I love the mask?'

Their faces set like thunder,
   The men with gravitas,
The men whose gold I plunder
   Each time I play the ass —

Too late they learn their danger
   In breach of fortune's rule,
That Lady Luck's a stranger
   To pride, but loves a fool.

[SOHO]

[120]

Chinese Whispers

[On looking into a dozen anthologised versions of
'On First Looking Into Chapman's Homer' by John Keats]

A comma here, a comma there,
Apostrophes inserted;
The stanza split to make a fit,
Indented lines inverted.

A semicolon gone astray,
And here, its tail deleted;
A second 'n' in Darien,
The error then repeated.

Ah, publishers are hasty men
Who like their bread with honey;
To proof a rhyme demands one's time,
And time, dear sir, is money!

[DORSINGTON]

Knowing When To Go

Some go early — lucky them,
The eulogies are frightful;
Some expire, *cherchez la femme*,
With relatives grown spiteful.
Some go gently, two by two,
Simpatico forever,
Some cling on, like me and you,
Through any kind of weather.
Some go screaming in the dark
With demons dancing madly,
Some go witty, some go stark,
The damaged goods go gladly.
Some go sudden, swept away
Fiddling, fey, like Neros,
Some defiant, stags at bay,
The way of unsung heroes.
Some, like cats, creep out alone
To join their feral brothers.
Some are gone before they're grown
To break the hearts of mothers.
Some go vicious, some go wise,
The saddest like a robot,
The best with starlight in their eyes —
Though where they go, I know not.

[MUSTIQUE]

Cause and Effect

['...what is found in the effect is already in the cause.'
— Henri Bergson L'Évolution Criétrice]

A wayward pebble clatters down the scree:
A minute later roars the avalanche.
A beetle buries eggs within a branch:
A decade passes; falls the stricken tree.
A microscopic virus in the breath:
A deadly battle waged within the veins.
A fungal spore mutates and famine reigns.
A word misspoke and comes a lover's death.
A poet makes a pass at someone's wife:
A fumbled gene aborted in the dawn.
A moment's hesitation with the knife:
A limbless Michelangelo is born.
A billion years without a sign of life:
A whisper from the gods— amoeba spawn.

[MUSTIQUE]

Marchesa Casati's Party

Marchesa Casati is holding a party,
It's terribly arty with Nubian slaves
And boa constrictors as luminous fixtures,
Draped upon pictures of virgins in caves.

The cost is colossal, her husband's a fossil,
A recent apostle of avant-garde art;
Though supra-exotic and faintly erotic
I hear she's neurotic and given to fart.

Her crows are albino, imported from Reno,
The leopard's called Fino, he's terribly brave
And once ate a flunky dressed up as a monkey...
Or was it a junkie who wouldn't behave?

Her jewels are Nirvana, she rides Lippizaner
And slips live piranha in gentlemen's beer,
She's sadomachismo and fondles a gizmo,
God knows what it is, though I have an idea.

Her set is precocious, her pets are ferocious,
Her guests are atrocious and some of them low;
Marchesa Casati is holding a party,
It's terribly arty — I think I shall go!

[DORSINGTON]

Marchesa Luisa Casati thrived in Rome in the early 1900's. Her hair was dyed orange framing a ghostly face adorned with mascara terminating in two-inch long eyelashes. She was a recluse for much of her life but gave fabulous parties which shamed and enraged her rivals. Her hobbies included encouraging avant-garde artists and keeping a menagerie of exotic and often dangerous pets. Spending more than one fortune without apparent restraint, she ended up penniless in London where, according to Lord Berner's biographer, Marc Amory, 'she showed uncomplaining courage.' I have embellished a little in my verse (I do not know anything about her husband(s)) but not by much, I suspect. Modern day goths and punks — on you knees!

Sex With Your Ex

Less guilt,
Less wilt,

Less nag;
More shag.

[NEW YORK]

From the headline brain-storming session for the December 2001 edition of *Stuff* magazine, edited by Greg Gutfeld in NYC.

The World's Last Choir

And so they came, the living and the dead;
Quiet, unconcerned with their condition
Or their status, by love of music led,
Each lover of his separate volition,
The rope of lies too short to warp their way.
They sung at no command, their throats combined,
A mighty host whose dust would dark the day
Were such dust present; the sighted and the blind,
The halt, the lame and those whose flesh had long
Since passed into the mystery of song.
In fugal thrall, bound up by chords of praise
They sung the waning law of earthly days
In unison, their voices ever higher
On that last day, and they — the world's last choir.

[NEW YORK]

Fast Awake

When I was young I fell asleep
  And dreamt I sailed upon a sea
Where dreams were real enough, and cheap.
  We called the sea: *Reality.*

The colours of the world have leached,
  My skin is creased, my fingers shake;
I woke to find the barky beached.
  Spiced foods give me the belly-ache.

I wonder if I'm fast awake
  Or dreaming still? I wouldn't know.
The sea is shrunk into a lake —
  And where did all the mermaids go?

[SOHO]

'Mighty the ant to an aphid...'

Mighty the ant to an aphid,
  Mighty the spider to fly,
Mighty the tiger to bullock,
  Mighty the mink to a nye;

Mighty the urchin to beetle,
  Mighty the fox to a foal,
Mighty the cuckoo to robin,
  Mighty the hawk to a vole.

Mighty the weasel to coney,
  Mighty the wolf to a dog,
Mighty the lion to jackal,
  Mighty the jackal to hog;

Mighty the bailiff to peasant,
  Mighty the power of the pen,
Yet, mightier, love,
    than all the above
  Is the tongue of a woman
    — to men!

[35,000 FEET MID ATLANTIC]

[127]

French Connection

[for M-F]

We do not speak as lovers,
Nor hold each other's hand;
We give no sign to others,
To help them understand.
Nor have we planned
To meet each other's mothers.

I play the ukulele,
She solos in the choir;
Our countries quarrel daily
And call each other liar.
And yet the fire
Burns brightly— even gaily.

I tell her, 'I adore you,'
She pouts and pokes her tongue.
Well, that's French women for you,
But once the harp is strung
No song is sung
More gently to restore you.

I sit and write my verses,
She sips a glass of wine
And shrugs at grumpy curses,
She's here in every line;
This book of mine
Is graced by her sweet mercies.

[DORSINGTON]

Ed
[Tombstone for Ed Barker]

Ed, you silly bugger!
Damn your woolly hide,
What d'yer think yer playin' at?
Annie, stand aside!
Rouse yourself now Eddie!
Draw me something, son!

Barker! Are you listenin'?
Annie! Christ, he's gone!
Run away and left us,
Kiboshed! Bought the farm!
Ed, you had it all, lad,
Ripcord looks and charm,

Razor wit and talent.
I can't believe you're dead.
Pardon me for asking...

...Why'd you do it,
                    Ed?

[MUSTIQUE]

The death of any friend is painful. That of Edward Barker, a soft-eyed, quick-witted, one-off-the-wrist cartoonist of immense likability and charm still bewilders and angers me in equal measure. Ed drank himself to death. But why? We bought Ed his 'last supper' consisting of every forbidden food known to man (I recall *foie gras*, olives, salami, oysters and lager) at his hospital bed. His doctors told us it didn't matter anymore what he ate or drank. I ranted at him for a minute or two as described above (Annie is a *nom de guerre*, by the way) but received only a knowing wink and a smart-arse reply for my pains. He died not long afterwards. Why, Ed? Why?

To A Beautiful Lady
of a Certain Age

Lady, lady do not weep —
What is gone is gone. Now sleep.
Turn your pillow, dry your tears,
Count thy sheep and not thy years.

Nothing good can come of this.
Time rules all, my dearest, 'tis
But folly to be waging war
On one who never lost before.

Lady, this is all in vain,
Youth can never come again;
We have drunk the summer wine,
None can make a stitch in time.

Nip and tuck 'til crack of doom,
What is foretold in the womb
May not be forsworn with gold —
Nor may time be bought or sold.

Dearest, do I love thee less,
Do I shrink from thy caress?
Think you I could cease to care?
Never was there one so fair!

Lady, lady do not weep —
What is gone is gone. Now sleep.
Lean against me, calm your fears,
Count thy blessings, not thy years.

[MUSTIQUE]

If all commercially minded cosmetic surgeons were tied end to end along a railway track — that
would be me stoking the train without a qualm in the world.

'If death knows no dominion...'

If death knows no dominion,
    The dead wield iron claws:
Ghost limbs aligned to pinion,
    To bend us to their cause.

By hoary yews and birches
    We worship gods they chose;
We sweep their empty churches,
    We smite their ancient foes.

If death knows no dimension,
    The dead are with us still;
By custom — and convention,
    They wed us to their will.

Their art a thing of beauty,
    The bait by which we're led;
Little we bring but duty
    To serve the ghastly dead.

[NEW YORK]

Written after reading 'And Death Shall Have No Dominion' by Dylan Thomas one fine fall night having just viewed the surreal wreckage of The World Trade Center under arc lights. Surreal or not, I was shaken to the core at the horrifying evidence of how history binds us all in the chains of old hatreds and mutual loathing. Dylan Thomase died a few blocks from where I wrote the above lines.

Surreal Deal

[And the Devil whoops as he whooped of old:
'It's clever, but is it Art?' — Rudyard Kipling]

I fixed the lion-bicycle
And fed the furry cup;
I polished Marcel's urinal,
(Some Mutt had blocked it up).

I used the lobster telephone
To call my Dada's brute,
But Salvador was not at home
And Isidore was mute.

Magritte told me a secret when
I mentioned André's twins:
He told me they had eaten them
To wash away their sins.

I don't believe those babies died,
I've heard they're still around,
Installing bricks for Maldehyde —
And charging by the pound!

[DORSINGTON]

Aleister

['Do what thou wilt shall be the whole of the Law.'
— A. Crowley The Book of the Law (1909)]

Aleister did what he wilt,
But it wasn't the whole of the law;
(Once you eradicate guilt
Banality takes to the floor).

Charlatans loathe what they build,
They leave their disciples to rot;
Aleister did what he willed,
But smashed all the toys in his cot.

Aleister's calling on Thoth,
While pentagrams hiss on the floor;
He's raising the demons of wrath —
But nobody cares anymore.

[DORSINGTON]

Crowley was a diabolist and self-styled magician during the late 19th century magical revival in Britain. He liked to be described as 'The Great Beast' or 'The Wickedest Man Alive' and went by the numerical pseudonym '666'. Utterly besotted with his own notoriety, he filled newspapers of the time with stories of drugs, orgies and sacrificial rites. A prolific but feeble poet, he was a member of The Order of the Golden Dawn along with W B Yeats, but left after a row about his cabalistic status. Think of him as a slightly less vicious, better educated and bald version of Charlie Manson and you won't be far wrong.

A Norman Priest Dreams of the English

How now, this cross-grained mongrel breed
Of foul-mouthed curs — thieves all! — their tongue
A sticky coil of stolen dung,
Who, ceaseless, on their betters feed;
And like some choking, noxious weed
Run riot where once roses sprung,
Their hybrid coarseness careless flung
On silk hard won by word and deed.
They nothing know but where to strike
Their enemies, these pearl-struck swine
Who piss in fountains, foul oaths hurled
At slattern wench or priest alike.
And yet! I dreamt a dream. a sign!
These oafs — Sweet Christ! — will rule the world!

[DORSINGTON]

The Shield of Art

All art deceives — the mind if not the eye;
A finger pointing at the moon, confused
With lunar beauty. Thus is nature used
To cross the 't' in Art and dot the 'i'
In Hubris. Spelt with a capital 'A',
'tongue-tied by Authority', suspended
To impress, (and, yes, the pun intended).
Yet art is not a thing. It is the way
By which men may reveal themselves as gods,
Arresting time. Made mad with loveliness,
The commonplace sublime, our craft sure signs
That though the Truth lays on with bloody rods
Men may endure; and as they groan, confess
Their Art is but a shield — as are these lines!

[52,000 FEET]

*Suggested by Nietzsche: 'We have Art in that we may not perish
from the Truth'. The phrase 'tongue-tied by Authority' comes from
Shakespeare, Sonnet lxvi*

'What time is it?'

The sands of time
   Race through the glass
As gravity requires,
  Each grain a mime
    Of dusty farce,
A silent rain of liars.

  The child at play,
    The man condemned,
New lovers at their pleasure;
  To such the sway
    Of time is hemmed
In grudging miser's measure.

  The child at school,
    The lover spurned,
The galley slave who cowers;
  Watch now the rule
    Of time upturned
As minutes pass like hours.

  'What time is it?'
    Who knows? Not I,
As Father Time — that traitor!
  The stars have writ
    His true reply:
'Much later — always later.'

[MUSTIQUE]

On Reading Dead Rhymers

I read the Hound of Heaven aloud
  and sought to catch my breath;
    Here Dead Lie We ashamed my craven heart.
Proud Raleigh's Even Such is Time
  swapped blasphemies with death.
    Wise Landor stood, full ready to depart.

In fright I fled from That Good Night,
  a wailing mere to sail;
    then crawled, appalled to cross the moaning bar;
Near spent, I entered Shelley's peace
  by way of Reading Gaol —
    at Charlotte's muse, I crossed a bridge too far.

*

'Enough, enough!' my lover cried;
  'Cease now and come to bed.'
    I marked my place but cannot face
  the lines I have not read —
  the unQuick on the Dead.

[DORSINGTON]

Because

Because men's pride is stronger than their purpose
 When pride is all they have, or all they've known,
Because the praise of neighbours makes us nervous
 (For men are what they are, not what they own);
Because our tinsel trrappings drive us blindly
 And 'way leads on to way' — and habits stick;
Because we love success — but not too kindly,
 And seek her out, but fear to learn the trick;

Because our lives are short — yet complicated,
 And all our wars are laid away on file,
Because our whims and sins are automated,
 Or buried in the tyranny of style;
Because there are no secrets worth the keeping
 And Keepers claim the Fifth — if ever pressed;
Because the Fourth Estate is busy sleeping,
 (An advertiser clutched to either breast);

Because the wolves of law are smooth-tongued liars
 Whose pimps in sober clothing fleece the flock;
Because our bandaged hands still stoke the fires,
 While Justice slips bright guineas in her frock;
Because our Men of God are — politicians,
 Who render unto Caesar what is due;
Because we fill our children with ambitions
 To mirror what we say — not what we do;

Because we shield our eyes from other's loathing,
 And hide away the follies of our youth,
Because we buy the label — not the clothing,
 And substitute good manners for the truth;
Because we mourn the crowd, yet shun seclusion
 For fear a voice may whisper what we're worth —
Because men damn free will to mere illusion:
 We walk those paths predestined from our birth.

[MUSTIQUE]

[140]

Mother Earth

Do not *trouble* yourselves on my account,
Nor put on airs, nor rave alone;
The teeth that snap,
The lips that flap,
The fist that shakes, I bred in the bone.
And your mother's heart is hard as stone.

Do not *trouble* yourselves with right or wrong,
For yours is not the only law;
The urge to blame,
The rage of shame
Has brought your house to peril's door.
And your mother forgave you, long before.

Do not *trouble* yourselves with shibboleths,
Nor seek to mend in blind despair;
The damage wrought
Is less than nought,
The price is more than a child could bear.
And your mother has long since ceased to care.

*

Envoi:

I *forgive!*
(And you will forget — anon).
Look up!
The stars! *Now get you gone!*

[MUSTIQUE]

Those who believe mankind capable of destroying the earth are, in my opinion, blinded by human self-importance. Certainly we are capable of making life on this planet uncomfortable, or impossible, for ourselves. But our influence pretty much stops there. Even if man were to loose every thermonuclear weapon he possessed, within a million or so years the planet would be crawling with diverse life forms. Within five or ten million years, it might prove difficult to detect any vestige of such a catastrophe. And, after all, five or ten million years is an eye blink in the measureless aeons the earth has supported life. As to the 'envoi', it is what I suspect will happen, providing we give ourselves sufficient time to 'escape' from our mother planet — a thought which, on the face of it, is mad. Yet it represents but a complex extension of the migrations that have ruled the development of all species of life on the blue planet.

Dead Gods

'When smashing monuments, save the pedestals — they always
come in handy.' — Stanislaw Lec Unkempt Thoughts

Some thirty thousand gods on earth we find,
Subjects of Zeus, the guardians of mankind. — Hesiod

'Thou shalt have no other gods before me.'
(You note the plural usage — lower case?)
Thus the God of Hebrews, wreathed in glory,
Set wrath in stone to chide his chosen race.

'Twas ever thus, in manuscript or mural,
The gods command and trembling men obey.
Yet often I have pondered on that plural:
The deathless gods — the gods of yesterday.

Who prays to feathered serpent, Quetzalcoatl?
Who to one-eyed Woden, lord of war?
Who praises Bacchus, god of flask and bottle?
Who mourns for Set or lusting Belphegor?

Who sacrifices meat in Chac-Mool's bowl,
Or bows to humble Hestia in her home?
Who worships Baal with fervent heart and soul?
Do not the sons of Isis rot, unknown?

Astarte waits in vain for mortal prayers
While eight-armed Kali counts her grinning skulls.
Dread Thoth is but a carving on the stairs;
The brass bull Mithras tarnishes and dulls.

Beneath the earth, in fetid catacombs
Lie empty altars, flecked in gold and mud;
My friend, I tell you, once, within those rooms,
Lived mighty gods paid out in lives and blood —

Blood that ran in temples, pooling, seeping,
Gouting from the knives of stone-eyed priests,
Blood of sons and daughters, slack-jawed, weeping,
Slaughtered where they stood, like craven beasts.

And now the lamb of Bethlehem has brought us
The meaning of His Word — yet iron rods
Still bind the mind. All history has taught us
To curse the names of thirty-thousand gods.

Immortals they were called, yet puny man
Still strides the world, their dust beneath his feet.
Let scholars sniff them out as best they can.
I spit upon their graves. Revenge is sweet.

[MUSTIQUE]

'They trouble sleep...'

They trouble sleep, the shadows of the past;
    Thus Magna Carta gnaws at tyrant schemes
While shadows of the present, slantly cast,
    Are what we call the future — in our dreams.

[DORSINGTON]

Last Supper

I once shared a cell with Mandela,
(Would you care for a leg or the rump?)
You'll remember that Maxwell feller?
It was me who convinced him to jump.

I spent a whole year as a hermit
In a trance in a cave in Ubud,
The llama himself will confirm it,
I was praying as hard as I could.

My climb up the face of the Eiger
Is a record, I think, that still stands.
I've spat in the eye of a tyger
As I finished him off with my hands.

I tutored Bruce Lee in ju-jitsu,
And invented the catamaran;
It's only much later it hits you
When you're living as hard as you can.

As for that bloody fool Geller,
He couldn't play poker for squat;
Though he knotted my Parker propeller,
I took every spoon that he'd got.

You may think Madonna's a lulu,
But I'm telling you now, man to man,
When your dick's being gripped by a Zulu,
You'll be coming as hard as you can.

(The corkscrew's behind you, young feller),
This Pétrus is all that I've got,
We're making a dent in the cellar,
But I'm damned if I'll leave it to rot.

They tell me I'm riddled with cancer,
So I'm planning to croak with élan,
If you'll pass the cigars and decanter
I'll be dying as hard as I can.

[DORSINGTON]

Most of us have met raconteurs similar to my hero above. You know that half of what they're telling you is untrue and that the other half is greatly exaggerated. But not knowing which half is which you say nothing and sip your cognac. The world would be a much sadder place without such rascals. In the words of Oscar Wilde; 'The aim of the liar is simply to charm, to delight, to give pleasure. He is the very basis of civilised society.' The particular gentleman I had in mind when I wrote this always used to part from dinner companions with a wink while saying: 'It's all good fun if you don't weaken.' So far as I know he never did, right to the end.

"Freeze!"

Thus consolation finds philosophers
Whose muddy paints obscure stark blacks and whites;
Yet when their houses fill with officers,
Guns drawn, the patterns shift to wrongs and rights.

[MUSTIQUE]

Green-eyed Monsters

Lad, poets write of love and loss
   In sober verse as makes no sense;
It's sugar-coated candyfloss!
   Truth is, they've no experience!

That 'starving artist' line's a fake;
   They're, most of 'em, just bags of wind.
Their blank verse gives me belly-ache,
   And half of them have never sinned!

Son, I've earned more inside a year
   Than fifty poets. God be blessed,
I hosed the lot on girls and beer
   And squandered nearly all the rest.

And now it's gone, who's left to care?
   Drink up! Before the Reaper calls.
Ignore the green-eyed monster's stare —
   There's damn few inns in Hades' halls!

[DORSINGTON]

Xanadu!

I'm certain she weren't from Porlock,
No more'n from Azerbaijan;
If only I'd fastened me door lock —
(It's murder to rhyme Kubla Khan).

There's times when a man needs amusin',
Lord knows I ain't made outta wood;
But rhymin' while lovin's confusin' —
And niever comes out like it should.

She stormed from me flat like a vandal,
But, Sam, I'm immune to 'er tears,
I think it's a bloody great scandal
Leavin' it two-'undred years.

Jinxed as a Jonah or jammy,
There's nuffin' a man canna' do;
I'm drunk on the milk of it, Sammy!
I'm finishin' off Xanadu!

[MUSTIQUE]

The story of Samuel Taylor Coleridge and the writing of 'Kubla Khan' has been told many times. In 1797, having retired to a lonely farmhouse on Exmoor, Coleridge awoke from a laudanum induced sleep. Seizing pen, ink and paper, he began feverishly scrawling the famous words: 'In Xanadu did Kubla Khan...' Regrettably, he was 'called out' before completing fifty lines 'by a person on business from Porlock'. When he returned to his room an hour later he discovered, to his utter mortification, that while he retained some vague recollection of his vision, he could only complete a further eight or ten lines, petering out on: 'For he on honey-dew hath fed, / And drunk the milk of Paradise.' Thus has 'the person from Porlock' entered the canon of English literature in odium.

Breakfast on Mustique

Ghost koi, their sunflower-yellow button eyes
Unstitched, weave shadows in the morning sun
And suck on moss-backed stones. The tree ants run
Amok, their only thought to tyrannise
Some hapless aphid. Scab-red dragon-flies
Patrol just out of reach, jaws set to stun
Their careless prey and drain them, one by one.
Night lilies fold away amidst the cries
Of Bequia-sweets at table, sword-sharp beaks
Extended — each scrap of food defended
From its neighbour. A tortoise heaves and wins
First prize: hibiscus flowers! Our kitten sneaks
Some bacon. The hungry night has ended;
Another day in Paradise begins.

[MUSTIQUE]

Ghost koi are are a pure silver-white variety of ornamental fish. The Japanese call them
Hikarimono or Ogon. Bequia -sweets (*Quiscalus lugubris*) are a form of Carib Grackle, common
throughout the Lesser Antilles. Sharp-eyed, bold and abusive, they squabble interminably.
Bequia, an island close by Mustique, is pronounced 'beckway'.

The Cremation of Jesus Christ

Caelan Fields, Llantrisant, Wales
January 13, 1884

Now stands the Old One, proud, on Caelan Field,
His Druid robe a symbol of his will,
The reek of burning flesh a righteous shield
As grim-faced farmers labour up the hill.

His outstretched arms a silhouette of fire,
He chants in Celtic tongue: "Thus sacrificed,
I now commend unto this funeral pyre
The body of my son, called Jesus Christ!"

His voice rings out in agony and pain;
A burly smith sneers up at him and spits.
The black smoke roils across the sodden plain.
A farmers jeers: "The devil's lost his wits!"

Alone, beside the flames, bereft of hope,
He hurls an errant brand in fiery arc.
Enraged, the screaming mob storms up the slope,
Their brutish faces shining in the dark.

"The land is for the living, not the dead!"
The Druid mocks, "You have no business here!"
"Foul blasphemy!" The single cry is fed
By half a hundred throats as they draw near.

"Not so, you misbegotten Chapel wights —
For those who bury men defile the land!
I choose the fires of old, the ancient rites.
Begone! Or would you kill me where I stand?

"And was it I who saved your wretched lives
When pestilence had laid the village low?
And was it I who visited your wives
In childbirth? Well, was it I, or no?"

A rotten log explodes upon the mound
In showering sparks. The furnace roars anew.
The ragged mob has reached the level ground:
Their leaders halt. The Old One points: "And you!

"Did not I save your daughter when the crones
Abandoned hope — and she now in her prime?
And you! Your broken leg and jagged bones,
I healed them; if you limp, still you can climb!

"Yet I am sore distressed and filled with woe,
My infant son, whom I named Iseu Grist,
Has given up the Ghost. I watched him go.
Fine thanks to bare your teeth and shake your fist!

"Your Chapel *ministers* have urged you here;
Their only mandate — their *authority!*
I see they lead by *skulking* in the rear —
But what am I to them, or they to me?"

A man steps forth, his soot-streaked eyes ablaze,
A hammer in his hairy paw: "Thou liar!
I care not what some heathen Druid says —
'Tis blasphemy! Consign him to the fire!"

Rough hands reach out in earnest as a shrill
Cacophony of whistles pierce the air.
"Police! Police!" the leaping shadows fill
With uniforms —
    I'll end my story there!

* * *

What's that? You're like to lynch me 'less I tell
At least the Old One's fate? Let this suffice —
    Cremation was made legal. All was well.
        I wrote these lines to honour
                Dr. Price.

[MUSTIQUE]

This is a true story. With embellishments! A plaque on the wall of Zoar Chapel in Llantrisant Reads: 'This tablet was erected by the Federation of British Cremation Authorities, to commemorate the act of Dr. William Price, who cremated the body of his infant son on Caelan Fields. For this act he was indicted on 12th February, 1884, where he was acquitted by Mr. Justice Stephens, who adjudged that cremation was a legal act. Thus was legal sanction given to the practise of cremation.' An eccentric, brilliant and kindly doctor (one of the first to practise homeopathy and scrupulous cleanliness), an ex-Chartist who twice fled the authorities to France where he was forced to live in exile for many years and a believer in nudism, reincarnation, free-love and Druidism, Dr. Price was 83 when he narrowly avoided death on that fateful night. And, yes, his son was called Iseu Grist, Welsh for Jesus Christ. Sadly, Dr. Price does not merit even a note in major encyclopaedias today. His memory deserves better, although he must have many descendants if he was still siring children in his 80's!

'Neither A Lender...'

I do not lend them money now,
(Or very rarely, anyhow).
It saves a friend. And saves a row.

You'd be surprised where friendship ranks
With those who think their friends are banks.
There's far more bricks than roses, thanks!

By some contorted somersault
It all becomes 'your bloody fault'.
It took me years to call a halt.

Some think you mean, some think you shrewd,
Far better that they think you rude
Than suffer their ingratitude.

And wise the man who will not lend,
But in the dead of night will send
A gift. And thus, will save a friend.

[MUSTIQUE]

'I have a secret servant...'

I have a secret servant
   (My rivals knew I must!)
A loyal thing, and fervent,
   A daemon I can trust.

He sits upon my shoulder,
   Has sat there many a year,
With age, he grows much bolder,
   And whispers in my ear.

And oftentime he's jolly,
   Though if at all ignored
He urges me to folly
   To keep from growing bored.

And sometimes he's indignant,
   Pretending then to weep,
And twice he's grown malignant;
   More often, he's asleep.

But when he senses danger,
   Or fancies easy meat,
God help the hapless stranger
   Who feigns to trick or treat!

He'll take a prince's ransom,
   And dice it — lose or win!
He's small and dark and handsome;
   (He bid me put that in!)

His motto: 'Faster, faster!
    No! Take the other door!'
But which of us is master,
    I've never quite been sure.

Yet I'd not be without him,
    (Though daemons know no friend);
He tells me, (I don't doubt him),
    He'll be there — til the end.

[MUSTIQUE]

Sally Alice

Both rich and poor alike bless Sally Alice.
Oft sickly, still she winks her eye at death.
Her sainted feet tread tenement and palace,
Yet sadder woman never drew a breath.

So answer this: does virtue cleanse its chalice
Of common mirth — like cuckoos in a nest;
Or is it that our laughter, like our malice,
Is rage disguised — mere baggage to the blessed?

[CANDLEWOOD]

Two Plants

Two summer plants grew side by side,
The one grew strong, the other died.

'Too close,' I heard a gardener sigh,
'The yew hedge roots have sucked her dry.

Too late for new to take her place,
The first must shield the empty space.'

Two plants grew in a summer bed,
Then winter came — now both are dead.

[MUSTIQUE]

'The estuaries of hell...'

The estuaries of hell are wide;
   The barges (Satan's special pride)
Provide for those who wish to ride
   One way; for just as advertised
The ferries are all subsidised.

[MUSTIQUE]

Blues

I found my South Side Mecca
By way of Ruislip Mews,
On Parlophone and Decca
Where white boys played the blues.

I spent my spare time lurking
Back stage to pay my dues,
I got my mojo working
With studs who played the blues.

I blew my education,
It wasn't hard to choose,
I passed my graduation
B-minus in the blues.

So if you hear me howlin'
Be sure to spread the news,
I'm howling for my darlin' —
I choose to sing the blues.

[MUSTIQUE]

The first and third lines of the last stanza are lifted almost verbatim from *Howlin' Wolf* (Chester Arthur Burnett) who, for me, represented the epitome of pre-war Mississippi-meets-Chicago blues. *Howlin' Wolf*, his 1962 Chess LP, (known as 'the rocking chair album' because of its cover art), helped to change the course of my life. It was difficult to imagine completing grammar school, going on to college and 'getting a job' after listening to tracks like 'Wang Dang Doodle' and 'Goin' Down Slow'. By my late teens, as a result of constant practice and heavy consumption of untipped French cigarettes, I found myself capable of a passable imitation of Wolf's voice. What audiences made of a half-demented, incomprehensible spotty git belting out 'Smokestack Lightning' and 'Evil Is Going On' in local pubs and clubs is quite another matter. One landlord told me frankly that, in his opinion, I came close to certifiable madness on stage. Looking back, I agree with him. I got laid a lot, though! Howlin' Wolf died in 1976.

'Within a maze...'

Within a maze,
    the path seems never-ending,
How many ways
    there are to lose one's way!
Yet from the air,
    in stately arcs descending,
Dark angels glare,
    impatient at delay.

By day and night
    we shamble, lost in beauty;
Turn left? Turn right?
    Or turn upon a priest?
The Minotaur
    performs his sullen duty;
Beyond the door
    The vultures hop — and feast.

[MUSTIQUE]

[158]

Grand-ma

Today he calls me 'grand-ma',
  My hair as white as snow,
But that's not what he called me
  Near fifty year ago;
My curls a fiery tangle,
  My skin a slick of sweat,
My lover riding bare-back
  And we just only met!

When next you're with your grand-ma,
  Try closing half an eye,
Smooth out the wrinkled creases,
  Add lipstick on the sly,
Imagine fiery tresses,
  Imagine there's no dress!
Then save your pity, dearie —
  Been there — done that. Oh yes!

[MUSTIQUE]

'So up my lads, we're glory bound,
The tide is turning on the Sound,
There's native girls with luscious lips
And nowt but grass upon their hips,
There's Spanish Dons, the old buffoons,
Their fat tubs stuffed with gold doubloons.
Strange stars there are in Southern skies —
Am I a man who'd tell you lies...?

* * *

Line up along Canary wharf:
Sign up to sail the *Bearded Dwarf!*'

[NEW YORK]

Dedicated with heartfelt thanks to all those shipmates who have toiled aboard the good ship *Dennis Publishing* these past 30 years. She's a fine barky, made finer still by the exceptional talent of the men and women who have crewed her, past and present. I never was much of a captain, I know that. But at least I had the sense to place her in seamanlike hands and retreat to the owner's cabin. (Well, for most of time, anyway!)

To cOpy-Editers

Pedants resistant to capital letters
Often will soften a point or erase
Barbaric italics to score off their betters —
Lucky for them i was born lower case!

[SOHO]

Whistling Ghosts

Bondsmen grizzled while they chiselled
*   Cleopatra's Needle;*
Cockneys warbled while they corbelled
*   Old St. Paul's Cathedral —*

Palaces with Grade I ranking
Once were scaffolding and planking;

Long before the hush of mourners
Workmen spat and shat in corners;

Monuments now called sublime
Were built with blooded sweat and grime;

In rooms which house our royalty
Whistling ghosts still boil their tea.

[SOHO]

Winds That Douse the Candle

If 'out of sight and out of mind' be true
How then may 'absence make the heart leap higher'?
Degrees of feeling reconcile the two:
The winds that douse the candle fan the fire.

[DORSINGTON]

Life Support

*[With breathless thanks to the staff of
Danbury Hospital, Connecticut]*

Upon a bed of ice and fire,
  I waited, swathed in tube and wire,
    My lungs a searing funeral pyre;
      They asked me my religion — I was dying.
Prostrated in the fever's grip
  I watched an intravenous drip
    Pump ballast, then abandoned ship;
      'He's sinking!' cried a nurse. I thought: *I'm flying!*

Much later, while I convalesced
  I learned what I'd already guessed,
    When on his rounds, a quack confessed:
      'We nearly lost you, son. You just weren't trying.
I've seen it once or twice before,
  You wandered through an open door
    But can't remember what you saw...?'
      'You're right,' I said. And found that I was crying.

[MUSTIQUE]

[166]

Bedtime Story

'I'll come to thee by moonlight, though hell should
bar the way!' — Alfred Noyes 'The Highwayman'

I was reading him 'The Highwayman'
As he lay tucked up in his bed,
My fingers drumming the horses hooves
On the back of the book as I read;
I read by a ribbon of moonlight
As he turned to me to say:
'I hope that he dodges the soldiers!
Though hell should bar his way!'
But I lost myself in that wild ride
Of a man in a velvet coat —
And when I looked he was fast asleep
With a bunch of sheet at his throat.

[SOHO]

'Love is not compassion...'

Love is not compassion, or a kindness,
   Nor is love attraction steeped in lust;
Friendship and affection lack its blindness:
   Such do as they can — love as it must.

[SOHO]

A World That Was Not There

I turned to find a world that was not there,
Its pages blank, the quisling air grown dumb;
No sign, no sign, all vanished in thin air.

I ransacked drawers and cupboards, all quite bare,
Each finger now had grown into a thumb;
I turned to find a world that was not there.

I stopped to catch my breath and say a prayer
But lost the thread before 'Thy Kingdom come';
No sign, no sign, all vanished in thin air.

I glanced into a mirror in despair,
My lips were mouthing out 'fee fi fo fum';
I turned to find a world that was not there.

I panicked, fled the room and down the stair,
Outside, no trumpets blared, no cymbaled drum;
No sign, no sign, all vanished in thin air.

I joined the throng of those who'd ceased to care,
Our memories now fading, hearts grown numb.
I turned to find a world that was not there;
No sign, no sign, all vanished in thin air.

[SOHO]

[168]

'Say this to thyself...'
[for W.E. Henley]

Say this to thyself (beneath thy breath,
　　But say it and have be done):
"A mortal's thoughts of dying and death
　　Are shadows across the sun."

Say this to thyself (come take some wine,
　　'Twas ever the coward's mark):
"There will come the time when I and mine
　　Must ferry into the dark."

Say this to thyself (or sing out loud,
　　And shatter the windy sky):
"Though sore afraid I shall not be cowed,
　　I *live* till the day I *die*."

Say this to thyself (but bail, my friend!
　　No boat stayed ever afloat):
"From this day forth to the bitter end
　　I shall seize life by the throat."

[DORSINGTON]

'No one ever sang more courageously of life than William Ernest Henley' wrote Louis Untermeyer. He lived much of his life in constant pain, crippled for the last forty years. But even after the death of his daughter he refused to succumb to self-pity and worked on, 'busy and belligerent'. Derided by serious critics of poetry for the sentiment (and, more unforgivably, the popularity) of his most famous poem 'Invictus', Henley spent most of his life as an editor. He made 'many gratifying discoveries among the younger writers.' His later poetry, especially the moving 'Margaritae Sorori', suggests that he might have done better to explore his own talents as a poet more fully.

Johnson

[for Robert L. Johnson]

I sat last night in Soho
    Blues falling down like hail,
The Devil in falsetto,
    A hellhound on his trail.

The words came helter-skelter,
    Long fingers fiddling fire,
Your soul is in the Delta,
    When Johnson bends the wire.

The say he bought tuition
    From Satan on the sly,
But that's just superstition;
    Still, when he came to die,

When Hell's lieutenant coshed him
    To take him fair and square,
I bet young Johnson joshed him:
    'You got guitars down there?'

[SOHO]

The first time I heard Robert Johnson (*King of the Delta Blues*) in 1966 on vinyl, the hair stood up on the back of my head. It still does. Here is talent and musical virtuosity made flesh, salted with hints of madness and voodoo intimations of mortality. He died in his middle twenties, his whisky poisoned, so they say, by a jealous rival. I once came across a quote concerning the worth of an artist's life (Keats in this case) measured against the lives of their contemporaries: "Ode on a Grecian Urn is worth any number of old ladies." Political correctness proscribes such elitist sentiment today, but Robert Johnson's genius could lead me into the shadow of temptation damn easily!

Old Dog, New Trick

I am an old dog which has learned a new trick
Concerning the secrets of sunlight. This trick
Will not improve one's pension
Or aid in the prevention
Of indignities to come when one grows sick —
Sick of a world grown sick of an old dog sick
Of being sick. But still, it is a *new* trick.

You must sit by quiet water, in the sun,
In the morning or the evening. Said sun
Must fall in such direction
As angles its reflection
From the water to your eye. This being done,
Squeeze both eyelids tightly shut. *This* being done,
Be still. There will come an image of the sun —

But in such colours! And there's a further trick:
Take a battered hat to wear. This added trick
Keeps diamond light from fading
While colours come cascading,
In cataracts. In a while you may feel sick —
Sick of a world grown sick of an old dog sick
Of being sick.   But still, it is a *new* trick.

[DORSINGTON]

Fundamentals

The fruits of the Crusaders haunt us still,
'Creationism' slithers from its hole,
They'd kill us all to save one mortal soul
While heathen unbelievers foot the bill.
Priest, wherein lies the freedom in 'free-will',
The gift of which was never yours to dole?
You but return to men what first you stole
With hints of paradise to coat the pill.
Your certainties speak love but end in death:
The mullahs bay for blood in Babylon,
In Bethlehem the Hebrews marshal tanks.
A pox on every martyr who drew breath —
Hard sermons do but urge the rabble on
While hooded sons of terror smirk their thanks.

[NEW YORK]

Charlotte

*[Time Future whispers in
Charlotte Mew's ear]*

There's ash a-plenty in London town,
Oh, Charlotte — stay your hand!
Retie those ribbons, put them down —
Your 'second-best' be damned.

A blemished pot, the clay misthrown?
Well, what are editors *for*?
Perfection lies with God alone —
Just toss them in a drawer.

A feminine rhyme grown scandalous,
It's veil beyond repair?
These midnight hours are perilous
For poets in despair.

Have done with pride, this urge to burn,
To tamper and to shred —
In fifty years the tide will turn;
Oh, Charlotte — go to bed!

[MUSTIQUE]

Less than sixty poems by Charlotte Mew survive — and yet we know she wrote many, many more.
Her life was plagued with unhappiness compounded by repressed sexuality and a fear of hereditary
insanity. Despite encouragement from one or two prominent poets, (Hardy called her 'the best
woman poet of our time'), her talent was generally unappreciated until after her suicide in 1928.
Worse still, Charlotte Mew's striving for perfection and, perhaps, her wish to conceal any trace of
lesbian eroticism, led her to destroy nearly all her 'second-best' work. Friends later claimed she had
'trunks full of them'. She was even reported as using these old manuscripts to light cigarettes from
the fire. For anyone who has ever read 'The Farmer's Wife' or 'I Have Been Through The Gates', this
represents a profound loss to English poetry. If you have not yet discovered Charlotte Mew, I envy you!

The Lamb Bids the Tyger Farewell

The poet has come to the pamphleteer
  Most secretly, most secretly,
The Lamb has spoke in the Tyger's ear:
  'I fear for thee. I fear for thee.

'The noose is looped on the Liberty Tree!
  A tyrant's rope, a tyrant's rope,
The Lion has loosed the Jackals. Flee!
  Thy only hope, thy only hope.'

The Tyger has taken the poet's arm
  His face is wry, his face is wry:
'And wilt thou come, O lamb of alarm?'
  'No, no, not I. No, no, not I.

'Oh, but I shall pen such a verse this day,
  To make amend, to make amend,
As shall shake the world in another way —
  Farewell, my friend; farewell, my friend.'

[NEW YORK]

In 1792, William Blake came to warn the fiercely radical activist and writer, Thomas Paine, that the British authorities were about to arrest him for treason following publication in London of the second part of Paine's *The Rights of Man*. Paine fled to Dover and took ship to France with the arrest party literally on his heels. Had they caught him, he would certainly have been hung — as his subsequent trial *in abstentia* made clear. Paine went on to take a significant role in the French revolution, just as he had in the American colonies, where his pamphlet, *Common Sense*, was influential in bringing about the Declaration of Independence. William Blake published *The Tyger* (Tyger, Tyger, burning bright / In the forests of the night...) in 1794 in *Songs of Experience*. Of course, the conceit that The Tyger in any way portrays Thomas Paine is merely that — as every scholar of Blake would affirm. Yet reading the poem again with the thought in mind made me wonder...

Of Walls and Fences

Of wrong or right I scorn to sing
(Philosophy pays less than pence),
I sing me of a little thing
Contemptible to common sense —
The rightness of a wall or fence.

If privacy is precious stuff
Then walls exclude a neighbour, true;
Except it puts them in a huff,
And, even worse, it spoils the view.
Such fences need maintaining, too.

Why envy what we cannot see?
But cant comes easy to the pen —
Men's lives are warped by property,
I've strung barbed wire, and will again.
A wall brings out the worst in men.

[MUSTIQUE]

The Weeds of Warwickshire

Their rotting bones lie scattered in each hedge;
I leant on one today and drank some beer,
Plucking at a rough leaf's double edge,
Conjuring the shade of what stood here

Before the beetle came, before the plague
Of death along each lane turned green to grey.
But memories are treacherous and vague,
Old photographs alone remain, today.

Armadas in full sail, fair emerald fleets,
The inshore squadron's glorious men-of-war,
Tall sentinels of shaded village streets,
Of warded pasture, hedge and cottage door.

'Elm Hateth man and Waiteth,' warn the crones,
'And all that walks upon two legs. Beware!
She'll Shed at nought to crush thy human bones;
Fey Fairy Queens Alone may shelter there.'

But elfin spell came never to their aid
As pestilence rained down in deadly tide,
And one by one those giants on parade
Succumbed to their peculiar suicide.

The Weeds of Warwickshire we called them once,
And shall again as centuries slide by —
These colonies of rotting stools and stumps
Will succour saplings blotting out the sky.

Man's span is short, his tribal lore truncate,
Yet *ulmus minor* flourishes below.
Within the dark her patient roots await
The passing of her parasitic foe.

[MUSTIQUE]

To human eyes, the onset of Dutch elm disease in Western Europe during the 1970's was a catastrophe. For elm trees, one suspects, it is a minor irritation, to be endured and overcome, just as it has been in the past and will be in the future. Elms are alive and well — flourishing even. It's just that we can't see them except as untidy shoots emerging from felled boles, 'testing the water', so to speak, for their parent roots and suckers which remain safe from the beetle in the sanctuary of the soil. And, yes, they did commit a form of suicide to combat this latest invasion, although arborealists will swiftly discount such notions as anthropomorphic nonsense. Well, perhaps. But it can't be denied that neither beetle or their pupae killed the elms. The Weeds of Warwickshire simply shut off their own sap and went underground, just as they have done in cycle after cycle for untold millennia.

Fin Finis

[A Shanty for a Harpooned Whale]

Haul away,
  Haul away,
    My proud bully boys, haul away.

A whale knows
  That you know
    As he knows
What only the prophets foresaw;
      When at Gaia's last turn,
      At entropy's burn —
Whales will walk as they once walked before.

Haul away,
  Haul away,
    My proud bully boys, haul away.

A whale dreams
  That you dream
    Of her dreams;
Of spume and of krill and of claw;
    Of cold Arctic moons,
    Of exploding harpoons —
And of fires that will crack the sea floor.

Haul away,
  Haul away,
    My proud bully boys, haul away.

Oh, two legs,
    Or four legs
        Or no legs,
The helix runs false at its core;
    As the sun slowly dies,
    As the boiling seas rise —
Whales will dance on the ocean's last shore.

Haul away,
    Haul away,
        My proud bully boys, haul away.

[DORSINGTON]

'A miser's purse...'

A miser's purse may nurse
    A poet's pen;
I've supped with pigs whose verse
    Would break your heart —
And slept with wall-eyed sluts
    Who spoke of Zen:
Men's lives are not their own,
    Still less their art.

[CANDLEWOOD]

A Hymn of Hate

[A British Sergeant Addresses His Squad
September 26, 1914: La Bassee Canal, France]

I won't trouble you with sermons,
    And we'll keep this short and sweet,
Men, we're 'ere to slaughter Germans,
    Here to mow 'em dahn like wheat,
Yes, to fight 'em and to kill 'em,
    For a Briton never bends,
And a bayinit's a weapon
    With a worker at both ends.

Kaiser Willy dines on babies,
    Deep be'ind the Belg'un lines,
Like a pack of dogs with rabies
    We must execute the swines,
We must root 'em out and kill 'em
    'Till they begs to make amends,
For a bayinit's a weapon
    With a worker at both ends.

Nah, there's pacifists out mouthin'
    That there's two sides to a coin,
(When the Hun march into Southend
    They'll be queuin' up to join!
Me? I'd lock 'em up and mock 'em),
    For our country nah depends
On its bayinits, a weapon
    With a worker at both ends.

For the Hun will grow no wiser
    'Til his armies are a wreck,
And we've 'ung the bleedin' Kaiser
    With a rope ahrand his neck,
And we'll stick 'im as we string 'im
    'Til the fat pig compre'ends
That a bayinit's a weapon,
    With a *whoreson* at both ends.

And it's filthy work we do 'ere,
    Though I do not make a daht,
That we'll all be 'ome by New Year
    Once we root the bastards aht,
Once we root 'em aht and kill 'em!
    That's the message England sends
From its bayinits, a weapon
    With a worker at both ends.

[NEW YORK]

Seek-no-further
[The Walking Apple Tree]

Down the hillsides of New England
Apple blossoms scent the air;
Seek-no-further farmers call 'em;
English settlers put 'em there.

Planted 'em high up the mountains,
Knowing 'em a tasty bite,
Knowing when an old tree rotted
It must fall one wintry night;

Knowing that its shoots and branches
Walk the hills and spring anew;
Seek-no-further farmers call 'em:
If you ate 'em, you would, too!

[DORSINGTON]

I first came across the story of *Seek-no-further* apple trees in Eric Sloane's book A *Reverence for Wood* published in 1965. According to Mr. Sloane, the first such tree was planted 'in the 1700's in Westfield, Massachusetts on top of Dudleytown Mountain' by an English settler who had brought the seeds from Cornwall. Over the centuries these trees, which have the habit of re-rooting their branches when they collapse from old age, have gradually crept down the slopes in various parts of New England, especially Pennsylvania. They are still to be found, sometimes known as Westfields. Until the early part of last century, farmers would occasionally take their family up into the mountains to graft Westfields onto wild crabs. If Mr. Sloane's folk-lore is true, there may well be apple trees in New England which, in a sense, are three hundred years old. It is a fancy of mine to bring back a handful of wild *Seek-no-further* seeds or layerings across the Atlantic and plant them here in England — on a hillside, of course!

Atlas Shrugs

As mass extinctions come and go,
    They sneer at Michelangelo;
Shakespeare's genius is just
    A rumour to volcanic dust.

Bacilli and fungal spores
    Lose no sleep on Newton's Laws;
Nor do polar ice-caps learn
    Of odes upon a Grecian Urn.

Neither moon nor asteroid
    Alters course for Jung or Freud;
Atlas shrugs and rolls his eyes
    When hairless apes philosophise.

[MUSTIQUE]

Swim or Float

Wise men advise we float the stream of life:
    "All folly lies in wishes unfulfilled."
It's clear that wise men never had a wife,
    Or ever poured a glass of Chablis — chilled!

[SOHO]

[185]

Sign To Be Erected
At The Gate To Argyle Wood

It ate you up. I know it did.
They used you, then they turned away.
They used Your Honour, then they hid
Their pretty little toys away.

They laughed at you. I heard them laugh.
Wrong tie; wrong club; wrong bloody school.
They never saw the better half.
I did. Now rest, you daft old fool.

Here's glory from your enemy
That never was, sir. God forbid.
They tricked you, but they shan't trick me.
It ate you up. I know it did.

[MUSTIQUE]

Michael Argyle was the judge at the OZ Trial held in Court Number 2 at The Old Bailey in the summer of 1971. Despite his highly partial summing up, the jury found my co-defendants and me not guilty of the only serious charge of which we were accused — 'Conspiracy to Pervert the Morals of the Young of the Realm'. Despite this, Argyle sentenced us to prison in what even *The Times* described as 'an act of establishment revenge'. That he had cocked up the longest 'obscenity' trial in British history (from the Establishment's point of view) was made abundantly clear by Lord Chief Justice Widgery's comments at the Court of Appeal some months later. Yet Argyle's treatment from the powers that be following this debacle was almost as shabby and dubious as the trial itself. They simply ignored and demoted him. Argyle was a victim, not a perpetrator. The simple truth is that he was selected as the OZ Trial judge because he was expendable. He will have a wood named after him within the forest of his 'enemy that never was', not in mockery, but as a memento from one victim to another. A bad judge, but not a bad man.

God Knows What

Much easier by far to shrug of course,
When some fool asks: Do you believe in God?
No river ever ran without a source —
I've always found the question rather odd.

Theology was writ by mortal men;
Their faith and funny hats are all they've got.
When all is said and done they rule by pen;
For certain something's there
              — but God knows what.

[MUSTIQUE]

Deducing Fairies

The tide of contradiction swirls and foams
    Unceasingly, lest mortal thought should harden;
What demons drove the don of Sherlock Holmes
    To fairies at the bottom of the garden?

[MUSTIQUE]

The simplistic answer to that question is the death of Sir Arthur Conan Doyle's son from wounds incurred in the First World War. Doyle's interest in spiritualism blossomed into an obsession which led him to support several charlatans, despite a public pose of scrupulous 'authentication' towards spiritualist claims. The 'fairies at the bottom of the garden' was one such case. Pictures of 'the little people' were cut out and photographed in a garden setting by mischievous children. For years their authenticity was a subject of serious debate. What the abrupt, analytical Holmes would have made of such nonsense is best left to the imagination. For me, however, Doyle is still the greatest writer of detective fiction who ever lived — and be damned to the fairies!

Neanderthal Nights

And if out walking on a summer's night
Up Coxcombe Hill, the stars for company,
A bellyfull of beer to comfort me,
I should chance to see in the bleached moonlight
One of the Old Ones, hairy, arms locked tight
Around some piggy-backed monstrosity
Perched upon her shoulder, loping casually
Across the Downs as if the ancient flight
Of all her kind was but an old wives' tale —
What then? Might I lie hid beside the trail,
My ferulled walking stick a flint-tipped spear?
Or should I step in view, supressing fear,
Professing brotherhood? (Not in this song:
I've read the Old One's memories were long!)

[MUSTIQUE]

'Though no good deed...'

Though no good deed escapes due punishment,
Yet kindness in a naughty world endures;
The ripples of its pebbled sediment
Betray the shoals that wickedness obscures.

[DORSINGTON]

Seven-legged Spider

Beside my desk there rests the noble NOD
Upon whose blue and silver spine this morn
I watched unfold a mystery of God,
A seven-legged spider squirming to be born —
Or should I say re-born — his useless husk
Discarded on the 'g' while he ran straight
Around the board into the shadowed dusk.
I counted out his legs, and there were eight
(Though one was but a nub — 'twill doubtless grow
When he at last emerges from his lair).
Is sacrifice, then, all we need to know
Of life's perfection? Gods of fire and air!
  I'd cast my midwife NOD into the brine
  To thus repair this crippled verse of mine.

[CANDLEWOOD]

The New Oxford Dictionary of English, (the **NOD**), is, to my mind, the best new single volume
dictionary of British English in print. For years, I had thought those husks of spiders occasionally
found in empty wastepaper bins were their desiccated bodies. Not so, apparently!   Like crabs,
some leave their dried out carapace behind in order to grow larger — or to replace a missing limb.

Telex Memories

The click of the keys as we hit 'em,
The smell as the paper unrolled,
The messages squeezed so we'd fit 'em,
The whine of the clutch as it scrolled;

The clatter of traffic incoming,
The heading 'Most Urgent - Reply',
The rattling, beeping and humming:
'Two minutes. Encoding. Stand By!'

[DORSINGTON]

Throughout the 1960's, 70's and well into the 80's, a telex (probably a Western Union model) was an indispensable piece of office kit. Long before computers migrated from air conditioned 'clean rooms' controlled by men in white coats to desk tops, the only sensible and secure method for a company to communicate long distances was by telex. Long distance telephone calls were ruinously expensive and air-mail post too slow. One would first reduce the message to the shortest possible length - often using code and jargon - then type it into a telex keyboard and finally push a button or pull a switch to send it to another telex machine, thousands of miles away. As the machines were electromechanical, one got used to their idiosyncrasies — rather like early cars which had to be started or driven in a certain way to ensure they worked at all. The message from a telex was printed out on rolls of paper (sometime coloured yellow) and requests for an immediate reply were common. It sounds almost pathetic now, but this feeling of being in communication with another person half way around the world was really exciting! The fax machine, of course, put telex communication out of business virtually overnight in most Western countries. I loved 'em!

The Old, Old Error

Think you — full certain all men must embark
    And slip their cabled moorings from this place
To journey, Christ knows where, upon the dark —
    That He will make exception, in your case?

[DORSINGTON]

The Snowman

He was sitting by the tow-path on a stump,
   Like a moonlit sihouette,
With the snow settling softly on his shoulders.
   'Bout eleven more mile, yet!'
He hailed, pointing with his pipe down river.
   Swinging the prow midstream
I spun the wheel to broach the white-flaked wind
   And brought her hard a-beam,
Kissed the jetty, cut the engines, grabbed a rope
   And reached to tie the cord
Around a ringbolt. 'I'll take that, you lubber,'
   Wheezed the snowman. 'Back aboard
And sling me down the other from the blunt end.'
   Ten minutes later we
Were sitting in the cabin, sipping tea. Outside
   The snow fell silently
And a frosted moon slipped in and out of clouds
   Fringed by nodding Norfolk reeds.
'I be the local ferryman' — so he told us:
   'Where the Great Black Mere feeds
The Yare, a ferry's stood for nigh five hundred year.'
   He bid us moor the night
If we should want, then gravely took his leave,
   A gaunt, archaic sight
With his oil-lit lantern bobbing through the gloom
   And a tread as soft...as soft...
Suddenly all the hairs on the back of my head
   Stood up and racing aloft

I found us floating free, the ropes limp down the sides,
  The 'jetty' but a spit of mud.
Gunning up the engines I reversed, half thrust,
  The fear fierce in my blood
And called our for a torch. We played it on the banks
  Amid the freezing air
But though we searched and searched and searched again
  There were no footprints there,
Nor ringbolts. In the pub that night at Yarmouth
  We asked a local at the inn
If he'd heard of a ferry by the Great Black Mere:
  'No,' he shrugged, with an evil grin.

[MUSTIQUE]

In Time of Doubt

Outcast stands my Bible on the shelf
Beside the prince of darkness there,
It leans as though to warm itself
Upon the bonfires of Voltaire.
And if I thought that Ferney's wraith
Could thus adjust such lack of faith
I'd pluck the pair and weigh them out:
The both for wit, but which for doubt?

[SOHO]

Ferney was the estate purchased by Voltaire in 1758
just over the French border from Geneva.

You!

*[Against all orders, Beelzebub, Lord of Flies and Satan's Chief Lieutenant,
visits the dreams of mortals soon to be his master's guest]*

You!   You grinning parasite!
    Lounging on your Hepplewhite,
    Sharpening your cut-glass vowels;
    Hell will revel in your howls
    While demons dine upon your bowels.
        I warrant you'll grin then a'right...
        (You've got until tomorrow night!)

You!   You windbag sycophant!
    Lord of blather, king of cant,
    Polishing your sly replies;
    Behold the altar of your lies!
    Here busy tongues are thick with flies
        And used — it rhymes with excellent...
        (Two days, you piece of excrement!)

You!   My little chickadee!
    My master's given you to me!
    Blabber mouthing smut and dirt,
    Wallowing in others' hurt;
    Immersed in worse, your lips will blurt
        And vomit gossip endlessly...
        (Three weeks, and then eternity!)

You!   Ah yes, the chosen few!
    Certain I cannot be true,
    Struggling to wake and shout:
    Hearken to the maggot doubt,
    Lest when your soul go walkabout
        You find what wiser prophets knew...
        (Beelzebub waits here for you!)

[CANDLEWOOD]

No-Man's Land

Here we all are in no-man's land,
The lame and the halt, the sick and the damned;

Tunnelling dirt, 'n' shovelling sand,
Here we all are in no-man's land;

Scissoring wire with a trembling hand,
The lame and the halt, the sick and the damned;

Swallowing hate like contraband,
Here we all are in no-man's land;

All the escape routes plotted and planned,
The lame and the halt, the sick and the damned;

Busy as bees
     On scabby knees,
          Nobody sees
               The rusty keys....

The guards long gone, the walls unmanned,
Here we all are in no-man's land;

The lame and the halt, the sick and the damned
Tunnelling dirt, 'n' shovelling sand.

[MUSTIQUE]

Lord North Instructs His Son and Heir...
[on the latter's 18th birthday]

And are we loved, my boy? And has the Pope
      Turned Protestant?   Do pigs spring wings to fly?
      Is there a man among us makes reply?
The lower orders dream of noosing rope
Around our barbered necks! They live in *hope,*
      While we live at our *ease.* You wonder why?
      I'll tell you then, the trick, and you may ply
Your adolescence scruples up the slope
      Of men's debate. The answer is that *fear,*
Dear boy — make note! — is stronger meat by far
      Than envy. Thus, the aristocracy
      Has ruled time out of mind. *Fear knows no peer!*
Forget this for an instant and our star
      Must sink into the swamp, DEMOCRACY!

....Who Replies Thirty Years Later
[by his fathers tomb]

And were you loved, my Lord? And was the price
      Sufficient for the ferryman to heed —
      Or sent you sullen surfs upon stampede
To storm the very gates of paradise?
I mean no disrespect. It must suffice
      That any son could conjure such a deed
      At such a time. I fear, my Lord, your seed
Is sadly sunk. The fire has met the ice
      And one suspects the breed is near extinct.
Times change, magnetic NORTH has turtled poles
      As rivers now run uphill to the weir.
      The Whigs have stared us out and we have blinked,
While merchant pigs defile the honour rolls —
      Truth is, my father dear, *this peer knows fear.*

[MUSTIQUE]

Classic Clichés

Why do lies come wrapped in tissues?
Who would push an open door?
Am I really 'Yours sincerely'
When we've never met before?

Why is elegance always classic?
Why is frost a man called Jack?
Who has ever begged your pardon?
See *what* monkey on your back?

Are *all* suspects armed and dangerous?
Where's this level paying-field?
When is the eleventh hour?
Are the fates of all men *sealed?*

Why do people say 'Don't go there'
When you've never left the room?
When were you last bored to tears?
Why must prophets foretell doom?

Ever seen a wood that's treeless?
Why is envy always green?
Why is life a bitch, you bastard?
Can the whole nine yards be seen?

What's it all about then, Alfie?
By and large, I'd have to say,
When the rock has met the hard place —
Leave no stone unturned — OK?

[SOHO]

Flower Power

[For Pearl Bicar]

Came the Friday — came the dragon
  Up the stairs with fire and broom:
'Rent is *late*, young man,' she scolded.
  What's this? *Flowers* in your room!'

On an impulse, feeling guilty,
  I plucked out a splendid bloom:
'Would you take these, Mrs. Harris,
  Take some flowers for your room?'

Half a weary life had flown by
  (Oh, but she remembered whom!)
Since a lad had brought her flowers,
  Pretty flowers for her room.

She forgave me, smiling oddly;
  Strange, how dragons cease to fume.
Off she marched to find fresh water
  For the flowers in her room.

*

Always look beneath the armour,
  Make a rule from womb to tomb:
Take the time to smell the roses,
  Keep some flowers in your room!

[SOHO]

Galileo's Dream

There came a voice in dreams, a mighty roar;
My soul grew wings and fled, in terror hurled
Across the airy margins of the world.
Thou See'st Now What None Ere Saw Before!

I clothed my dream in copper and in brass
By candlelight and many a weary day.
One star-filled night, I brushed my fears away
And trembling, placed my eye against the glass.

My first thought was: Alas, 'twas all for nought!
Mere darkness visible, then by degrees
The heavens opened! Dropping to my knees
I cried aloud: *Behold What God Hath Wrought!*

[MUSTIQUE]

Craft

Speak not to me of Craft as Art untaught,
What need the trowel to curtsey
to the brush?
A walk within an old cathedral's hush
Is worth all the Picassos
ever bought.

[MUSTIQUE]

The Worm at the End of the World

Coiled, a monstrous dragon sleeps,
Hoarding the earth in clawed embrace;
Breathless, deathless.

Insolent over his corpse there creeps
The countless mites of a mortal race;
Feckless, reckless.

Brazen, impatient of old wives' lies,
Building a world on scaled seams;
Feeding, breeding.

Waking, he opens bees-winged eyes,
Vexed to be torn from evil dreams;
Rumbling, grumbling.

Belching, flexing leathery limbs,
The worm erupts in fiery flight;
Roaring, soaring.

Oblivious, deaf to prayer or hymns,
He settles to hoard the endless night;
Voices? Noises?

Nothing.

[NEW YORK]

'The earth has a skin and that skin has diseases; one of its diseases is called man' - Friedrich Wilhelm Nietzsche.

Named after the Greek earth goddess, the Gaia hypothesis, was proposed by British scientist James Lovelock in the 1970's. Lovelock suggested that '...the Earth's living and nonliving systems form an inseparable whole, regulated and kept adapted for life by living organisms themselves.' This link between life and its environment, a commonplace now, seemed mind-boggling at the time and helped plant the seeds of the environmental movement. But there is a dark side to the Gaia hypothesis — the insidious idea of 'balance', that if only we can 'keep the balance' all will be (relatively) rosy here on the blue planet; that if only, rotten, life-sucking humans would behave themselves and stop wrecking the planet, everything will be OK.

Sadly, this is silly, if beguiling, nonsense. 'Nature' has only two laws, which, in essence, are one: Change and multiply. Obedience to the latter, through the mutation of natural selection, leads itself to more change. Thus mankind's 'pollution' of the earth is what we were 'selected' for in the first place. After all, pollution is nothing more than change. That poisonous sink in the Caspian Sea is where the next set of pond-life will likely mutate. The Earth is not here for our benefit — we have been produced for the Earth's. That the changes we make may lead to our destruction is neither here nor there.

Falling, falling
[September 11, 2001]

Mommy! Mommy! Come and see!
The lady says it's history
Falling on 'hew-man-ity'.
Mommy! Mommy! Come and see!

All the world is calling, calling;
All the world is falling, falling...

Mommy! Mommy! Please don't cry.
Things are falling from the sky,
Look! A man has learned to fly!
Mommy! Mommy! Please don't cry.

All the world is calling, calling,
All the world is falling, falling...

Mommy, who was that who called?
See where all the smoke has crawled!
Mommy! Look! The tower has falled!
Mommy, who was that who called?

All the world is calling, calling;
All the world is falling,
                    f
                  a
                  l
                    l
                      i
                        n
                        g

[DORSINGTON]

Index

Acknowledgements

Permission from Viking Penguin, a division of Penguin Books USA, to reprint Résumé by Dorothy Parker is gratefully acknowledged.

I have tested the patience and affection of close friends and colleagues, using them as guinea-pigs while reciting my poetry hot-off-the-laser-writer. Let me thank them all here unreservedly — especially Dick Pountain, Marion Hills, Don Atyeo, Sue Ready, Eric Shaw, Bud & Patsy Fisher, Robin Miller, Mick Farren, Sir Simon Hornby and Sir James Mitchell.

I owe heartfelt thanks to my editor, Simon Rae. Undaunted by bluster, immovable in the face of blandishments and susceptible only to reasoned argument and the odd glass of Bordeaux, his wise counsel has rescued me time and again. There is not a 'thee', 'thine', or 'thou' in A Glass Half Full that he has not attempted to excise!

Moni Manning somehow finds time from her legal practise to read every poem I write. Not to vet them legally, of course, but to comment from a very different perspective from my own— that of wife, mother and 'ordinary' person. I am very grateful for her enthusiasm and gentle mockery. She is no 'ordinary' person.

Stan and Elizabeth Clayton, who own Firefly Guest House in Mustique, first persuaded me to read my poetry in public. As I now do so at the drop of a hat, I am not certain how much of a favour they did the world, but it meant the world to me.

The team who helped me enter the arcane world of the spoken-word are listed within the CD jacket, but I must especially thank Gerry Healy and George Taylor for their patience and technical wizardry. My old friend Richard Adams came through on the cover design and Bill Sanderson on the illustrations.

As I have no literary agent, Gail Rebuck and Simon Master helped me to find a wonderful publisher, Sue Freestone, at Hutchinson. She has been a tower of strength to a bumbling amateur. And speaking of towers-of-strength, Michael Boyd and Fiona Lindsay from the Royal Shakespeare Company could not have been kinder as they persuaded me that I could stand in front of a huge audience reading my verse, surrounded by some of the best stage actors in the world, and not make a complete hash of it. They were right, too, that the RSC would pack the Swan Theatre that evening.

This American edition affords me the opportunity to thank those responsible for organising my tours and the production of this edition. Bruce Sawford and Steve Kotok headed up the tours in the UK and US respectively like the old pros they are. Mick,

Tom and Mark from Class Act humped and trucked and lit and sound-checked from Monterey to Glasgow. Patrick 'Why-can't-we-ever-get-a-decent hotel?' Song, from Volchok Consulting, did his magic on the giant projection screen.

Ian Leggett and Catherine Bishop handled the finances. This is not a job for the faint-hearted. *The Week* magazine was the sponsor for my US tour — which means that *The Week's* readers and advertisers are the ones I really have to thank. Alistair Ramsay and Stephen Colvin, CEO's of Dennis Publishing in the UK and the USA respectively, have put up cheerfully with their Chairman's tyrannical appropriation of designers, marketing and internet gurus and other personnel. I thank them and all the staff at Dennis Publishing, especially Justin Smith, Lance Ford and John Lagana.

My American business partners of over thirty years, Peter Godfrey and Robert Bartner, provided real encouragement for this book, demonstrating once again how lucky I was to meet up with them three decades ago. And, of course, nothing (in Britain or America) can be done without lawyers. My thanks, then, to Simons, Muirhead & Burton in London and Jacobs, DeBrauwere & Dehn in New York City.

Sarah Braben of The Braben Company in Britain and Drew Kerr and his team at Four Corners in New York have led me around (and, when I insisted, *into*) the minefield of media relations for many years. With me as a client they all deserve medals. The William Morris Agency came through in the clinch and the editors of *Maxim, Stuff* and *Blender* at Dennis Publishing astonished me with their literary insights, especially Keith Blanchard. The unflappable Caroline Rush and Alex Patrick oversaw the production of this edition and Mike Dunn redesigned it beautifully.

Australian film-maker, Fiona Prendergast, followed me around for weeks shooting a film of the tour called 'Did I Mention the Free Wine?' — and I only lost my temper once! The film is a knockout. (To see clips, go to www.felixdennis.com) My personal staff, Wendy Kasabian, David Bliss, Suzanne Price, Amy Tranter, Michael Hyman, Lloyd Warren , Cathy Galt, Toby Fisher and Sharon Islam have done everything from tucking their boss up in bed to piloting helicopters. Er, actually it was Castle Air who flew the helicopters and Key Air who provided the jet planes and crew. Bob Price was always cheering from the wings.

I wish to express my genuine thanks to Miramax Books and its ebullient Editor-in-Chief and CEO, Jonathan Burnham. It was an absolute pleasure arm-wrestling and debating the merits of individual poems with him. In addition, his talented colleagues have been as patient as saints teaching this tyro the ropes of American book tours and book launches.

Lastly, I owe a debt to the late Michael Nixon, who urged me to seek for 'What Lies Hidden'. I have tried, my old friend. I have truly tried.